Catherine Bailey has a degree in market. experience in strategic and operational marketing, including more than a dozen in the UK legal sector. She fully understands the needs of law firms and barristers' chambers ensuring they receive just the right mix of marketing required to secure new business and leverage from existing clients. Catherine has the depth of knowledge of the legal profession that truly sets her apart from other marketers.

Jennet Ingram has worked in the marketing field for eighteen years, fourteen of which have been within the legal industry for software suppliers, outsourced service providers, law firms and barristers' chambers. She's a member of the Chartered Institute of Marketing (CIM) and holds Chartered Marketer status, an accreditation gained in 2011 and maintained to this day through the CIM's ongoing CPD programme.

A Practical Guide to Marketing for Lawyers

2nd Edition

A Practical Guide to Marketing for Lawyers

2nd Edition

Catherine Bailey

Managing Director, Bar Marketing Limited

BA (Hons) Marketing & Engineering

Jennet Ingram

Marketing Consultant, Bar Marketing Limited

MA, MCIM, Chartered Marketer

Law Brief Publishing

Published 2018 by
Law Brief Publishing, an imprint of Law Brief Publishing Ltd
30 The Parks
Minehead
Somerset
TA24 8BT

www.lawbriefpublishing.com

Paperback: 978-1-911035-95-4

We dedicate this book to our families; Pete and Lauren; Steve, Fearne and Penny; thank you for your unwavering support and patience throughout the writing of this book.

Thanks also to the readers of our newsletters. Your interest in our monthly marketing insights is the reason this book has come to life!

PREFACE

A marketing-orientated philosophy is essential for any organisation eager for success. Generally speaking, the legal sector is steeped in tradition and hasn't been amongst the first to adopt a marketing focus.

However, the Legal Services Act 2007 changed all that. Suddenly the old partnership model was up against a new type of legal practice – alternative business structures – ran by profit-driven businesspeople. These owner-manager entrepreneurs recognise the pivotal role of marketing in the battle for market share. They've got their well-devised marketing strategies and they're not afraid to use them. Fail to put up a good fight in return and run the risk of losing your valued clients.

Of course, some would argue that a shift towards a marketing-focused stance would and should have happened anyway. After all, the new gener-ation of partners wants to maximise their firm's profits – and, therefore, their drawings – just like any other industry's senior leadership teams.

Whether the shift was consequential or inevitable is irrelevant. What matters is how legal service providers respond and adapt in order to compete with the best. This concept applies equally to law firms and bar-risters' chambers. The competition's toughening up in both of these marketplaces.

The problem, though, is this: lack of marketing expertise and lack of budget.

For the former, marketing's one of those roles that everyone thinks they can do but only a few truly can. So recruit the right people. The problems in recruiting the correct people lie in the lack of knowledge of what mar-keting is. Firms and chambers often don't understand what actually constitutes marketing and therefore they're unaware of the knowledge, skills and experience required of the candidates they're considering.

For the latter, you've got to be willing to invest funds into your marketing initiatives, particularly when times are hard and marketing monies are typ-ically the first to be cut in these circumstances. It's only by spending money on marketing that you're able to secure future work. Don't stop spending.

You might not be able to afford the same in-house marketing expertise and budget allocations of the heavyweights in your sector which is where this book comes in.

This isn't a book on marketing theory. There are plenty of well-stocked shelves in your local bookstore and library on the intricacies of theory. This book's different. It's a practical how-to guide giving step-by-step instructions on how to tackle the various components that together make up your marketing plan. You'll find everything from communication and events to social media and strategy formulation and more besides in the subsequent chapters.

This second edition contains a new chapter about GDPR which is new data protection legislation being introduced on 25th May 2018. As legal service providers, you'll appreciate more than anyone else how important it is that you stay on the right side of the law with your marketing activities. Tighter regulation in the form of GDPR places onerous responsibilities on marketers. We talk you through the reform and explain how to operate a compliant marketing function.

Finally, to satisfy your curiosity, in case you're wondering how this book came about, it was borne out of our monthly e-newsletters. You see, we run a company called Bar Marketing that specialises in all-things marketing for the legal profession. Each month we send our clients and prospects a series of bite-size tips on how to improve their marketing from which we receive resoundingly positive feedback, particularly from firms and sets that don't have access to marketing professionals in house. Thus, when we were asked to produce this guide, we felt that it would be of most use to those firms and sets that haven't invested a great deal in marketing in the past. Investing in marketing doesn't necessarily mean having to spend more, although that would certainly have a positive impact if invested wisely. It means getting more savvy with the funds available to you.

If this sounds right up your street, then read on!

Thank you for buying and thank you for reading. If, by following any of the advice contained thereon in you achieve a measurable return from your marketing investment, we'll have achieved our goal.

Good luck with your marketing campaigns and please keep an eye out for the second edition of this book which is already in progress because marketing's never static and what worked yesterday might need altering to meet the market demands of tomorrow.

Catherine Bailey
Jennet Ingram
March 2018

Contents

Chapter One   Strategy: The What, the Why and the How   1

Chapter Two   The Importance of Branding in Law   25

Chapter Three   Ensuring Successful Communications   37

Chapter Four   Social Media Strategies   57

Chapter Five   What Makes a Winning Website?   79

Chapter Six   Press, PR and Events Planning   95

Chapter Seven   The Importance of Design   123

Chapter Eight   Developing Clients and Acquiring Prospects   135

Chapter Nine   Managing Marketing Budgets   147

Chapter Ten   Preparing for GDPR   159

Chapter Eleven   Essential Checklists   171
    Marketing priorities checklist   171
    SWOT & PEST templates   173
    Marketing strategy checklist   175
    Brand guidelines checklist   176
    Emailer checklist   178
    Direct mail checklist   180
    Social media checklists   182
    Event checklist   184
    Invitation checklist   189
    Creating customer case studies   190
    Budget planning checklist   192

CHAPTER ONE
STRATEGY: THE WHAT,
THE WHY AND THE HOW

Quite simply, a strategy is the plan of attack an organisation puts in place in order to achieve their goals and objectives. An organisation will have a corporate strategy into which all the operational implementation strategies will feed. If they don't, the plan will fail. If the strategic goals of the organisation are not communicated to everyone in the organisation, the plan will fail. Likewise, if the members of the organisation don't buy into the strategic goals, the plan will fail.

It's therefore essential for a strategy to be clear, concise and communicated effectively.

Understanding your market, or prospective market, is fundamental to success. The UK legal market is evolving at an unprecedented rate. Consumers of legal services (both commercial and private client) are savvier than at any other time and they have a whole internet of information available to them. They are also increasingly intolerant of poor customer service.

You will need to understand what legal services they require, how they want them to be delivered and what they will be prepared to pay for them. Alongside this, you will need to understand your true cost base; what services are profitable, which are loss leaders and which should be removed from offer.

As a consequence, lawyers need to become more commercially aware and treat their firms / chambers as corporate entities delivering legal services in a manner the client expects, to time and cost effectively. In order to achieve this, they need to understand how they are currently preforming in the marketplace and how they compare to the competition.

That's what we'll cover in this chapter, specifically:-

- SWOT analysis: A 'how to' guide

- The difference between B2B and B2C marketing

- The rise of the ABS and new business models for the provision of legal services

- Differentiating your organisation

- Marketing strategies

- Core components of the marketing strategy

- Getting to grips with big data and analytics

- Developing effective marketing plans

- Marketing your services internationally

- Communicating value

SWOT analysis: A 'how to' guide

The marketing world loves its acronyms. SWOT's one of them. Standing for strengths, weaknesses, opportunities and threats, the SWOT analysis is an analytical framework used for strategic planning by identifying internal and external influences, both positive and negative.

The SWOT analysis can be carried out on a company, product / service, place, industry or person. From a chambers and law firm perspective, you could audit individual barristers / solicitors, particular area specialisms or your organisation as a whole.

Ultimately, a SWOT evaluates your company from all angles thereby removing any blind spots and allowing you to devise ways to capitalise on strengths, eliminate weaknesses, seize opportunities and combat threats. With these insights, you can make informed decisions about your future business plans.

The format of a SWOT analysis is a 2x2 matrix, as shown here:-

	HELPFUL (for your objective)	HARMFUL (for your objective)
INTERNAL (inside organisation)	Strengths • _____ • _____ • _____ • _____ • _____	Weaknesses • _____ • _____ • _____ • _____ • _____
EXTERNAL (outside organisation)	Opportunities • _____ • _____ • _____ • _____ • _____	Threats • _____ • _____ • _____ • _____ • _____

Factors for inclusion

Strengths and weaknesses are internal factors and tend to be in the present. Opportunities and threats are external factors and tend to be in the future. In the internal – or micro – environment, you need to look closely at factors within your chambers relating to:-

Human resources – people, board members, target population
Physical resources – location, building, equipment, infrastructure
Financial – sources of income, profitability
Activities and processes – programmes you run, systems you employ
Past experiences – building blocks for learning and success, your reputation in the community
Services – brands, pricing

In the external – or macro – environment, analyse factors stemming from outside forces such as:-

Future market trends in your areas of expertise
The economy and competition
Demographics – changes in the age, race, gender or culture of those you serve
Society and the physical environment
Politics and legislation
Local, national or international events

The best place to complete a SWOT analysis is during a workshop session or brainstorming meeting with input from all members of the management team.

Results

Once you've gathered your data, interpret your results and decide your obvious natural priorities. This can be anything from market penet-ration (striving to increase market share for particular services), market development (identifying new markets for existing services), service development (creating new services to existing markets) and diversific-ation (the riskiest strategy – developing new services for new markets). From these strategic options, create your objectives. Make them SMART (another acronym – specific, measurable, achievable, realistic and time-based).

Summary

A SWOT is a very flexible, but powerful, tool. Many organisations often use it alongside a PEST (political / legal, economic, social and technological) analysis to take a wider view of the business landscape.

So, don't rely on your instincts alone. Use the SWOT and PEST template for proactive thinking as an aid to strategic decision making.

The difference between B2B and B2C marketing

Unlike high street law firms, barristers' chambers have not (until recently) been too familiar with consumer marketing. However, the changes in the market mean that it's time for many chambers to properly embrace direct access by devising strategies to target this market.

It's no longer sufficient for chambers to rely upon repeat business from their instructing law firms. While this continued work itself isn't assured anyway, it also means they may be missing out on a lucrative trade with the public. However, before they take the plunge whole-heartedly, chambers need to make sure they have the capability in-house (or outsourced) to deal properly with the instructions direct access generates. Attempting direct access without the proper infra-structure or support services could seriously damage a long-built client service reputation!

For firms or chambers embarking on a new market or direction, a general review of your marketing plans is advisable. Where direct access is concerned, it's effectively the difference between business-to-business (B2B) and business-to-consumer (B2C) marketing.

'Marketing is marketing', you may well say. While this is true to some extent, after all, good marketing practices are transferrable between B2B and B2C disciplines, yet there are distinct differences which should be acknowledged.

The bottom line is that the difference between B2B and B2C marketing comes down to the buyers' needs and perspective about the purchase. Business buyers make rational buying decisions based on increasing profitability, reducing costs and enhancing productivity. Consumers make emotional buying decisions based on cost and quality.

B2B demands professional, sophisticated materials, testimonials, and other activities that build credibility and strengthen long-term relation-ships. B2C demands compelling materials that grow awareness of your firm or chambers, and project quality service and best price.

The rise of the ABS and new business models for the provision of legal services

Following the changes to the Legal Services Act there has been a flurry of firms and chambers looking to change the way they do business. It does raise the question 'do they believe that the new structures are a utopian answer to their problems?' or do they really appreciate that it will be a combination of structural change, attitude change and a commitment to concerted marketing efforts (by proper professionals) that will deliver the results they are looking for.

There appears to be a number of models emerging, some of which are explored below.

The 'one-stop-shop'

This model focuses on two distinct business areas; outsourcing for large corporates with fixed fees for multi-year contracts (previously done by panels) and event work which is usually one-off activity work (typically these are commercial law areas and not used for personal injury or criminal work).

The commercial sectors tend to be barrister led, giving the barrister the ability to select the right team of associates and support people for the job. The aim is to deliver a cost effective and efficient solution to the client's issue with the minimum overhead. The model permits them to add barristers when demand for specific areas of work increases and also permits them to decrease barristers as required. Public access issues are resolved by the involvement of a solicitor led section. This type of ABS is proving popular with US law firms that are used to a more integrated approach.

The fee-earner option

It's not fair to say that ABSs only deal with commercial law. Indeed there are a number of organisations that deal directly with members of the public and also the criminal justice system. The management structure of these companies usually comprises of barristers and a solicitor that enables them to provide traditional advocacy and litigation services direct to the public. It also gives them flexibility on how the practice is run and subsequently expanded (and contracted). For example, they can expand their service offering by hiring relevant fee earners who are then supervised by the solicitor partner.

Traditional with a twist

In a more traditional approach, some of the larger firms and chambers have re-evaluated their markets and have adapted their service offerings in order to move away from 'risk' areas and into more lucrative areas. For example, some have moved the focus of their criminal teams to white collar crime, cyber fraud, health and safety and financial services. As a result they have decreased their dependency on public funded work. At the same time, many of these organisations have invested in creating a brand for themselves and have added an international dimension to increase their business opportunities.

These organisations have found success by segmenting the business into practice areas, each with a unit head who controls the budget, business plan and growth strategy. Whilst many of the departments within the organisations remain interlinked and thus can leverage from each other's business ventures, should the opportunity for de-merger present itself, then much of the internal segregation work is already done. This approach is common practice in a large number of public and private companies where it is particularly attractive to private equity financers.

The supply chain option

With the banning of referral feels and the increased scrutiny of claims management companies, it was only a matter of time before an entity was created to maximise the opportunities these presented. And so we have seen the emergence of organisations set up by claims management companies with the specific purpose of becoming an ABS. Typically in these organisations, the management team includes solicitors and barristers, and thus provides public access. They leverage the 'barrister brand' in their marketing, playing on the public perception that barristers are more highly qualified than solicitors and thus hiring one gives better value for money and a higher quality of service.

The pay-as-you-go

A novel approach that aims to put client service at the heart of the organisation, this type of ABS breaks down the legal matter into a series of milestones, the achievement of each triggering client payment. This can obviously only work effectively with fixed price costing together with the abundant supply of legal talent, be that fee earners, solicitors or barristers prepared to work within that format keeping costs to a minimum.

The specialist

Niche ABSs typically comprise their management teams of a mix of barristers, solicitors and non-lawyers (for the financial management of the business). The advantages of the new structure for this type of ABS are greater flexibility in how they operate and speedier decision making. The disadvantages are an increase in record keeping and risk management, although this can be viewed as a means to increasing their client care. The flexibility of the new structure presents them with the ability to offer employed barrister positions for newly qualified practitioners alongside flexible remuneration packages for self-employed barristers (including dual practice arrangements) and partnerships (complete with profit share) for senior practitioners.

Whichever structure legal service providers decide to adopt, they will need to market their services effectively, to the right audience, at the right time, with the right messages. They need to identify their current strengths and which skills are transferable to more profitable areas. They will need to look at the market demand in those areas and the market saturation. They will need a realistic and deliverable plan for growth and they will need to deliver that plan on time and on budget.

Differentiating your organisation

In a marketplace saturated with legal service suppliers offering very similar wares, differentiation is the key to competitive advantage.

As we know, the legal market is becoming increasingly commoditised. The arrival of the new entrants and ABSs will continue to drive commoditisation as everyone vies for the same business with the same service offerings. The more a legal service is commoditised, the less monetary value it is worth. Price becomes the determining factor. Faced with this situation, legal service suppliers need to find ways to differentiate their services from the new entrants and also from other existing suppliers so that they can retain and grow their market share without detrimentally affecting price. They also need to do it now, before the "big brands" with mass marketing spend become too established.

So what is differentiation? Differentiation is the creation of a unique value. This unique value both attracts new and retains existing clients. It also raises barriers to competitors by encouraging purchase over others and creating brand loyalty. However, it's not easy to determine or implement. Differentiation takes a real understanding of client and market needs, of market forces and of your own chambers or firm's strengths and weaknesses. It also needs great leadership to implement.

There are a number of ways to differentiate. However, all can be categorised within three broad strategies: service innovation, client care or organisational effectiveness.

Service innovation

Service innovation refers to the organisation's ability to identify emerging issues and trends within their areas of expertise. I don't just mean the legal developments within those areas, but all developments that may influence that specific market sector. They need to understand the impact of these developments on their clients and potential clients. Regular communications through website, social media, newsletters, events and direct mail / email all help to position them as the market leader in the specific sector. Working with other complementary suppliers reinforces this perception and helps to keep competition at bay. In short it differentiates the organisation and provides a competitive advantage, assuming that they are ahead of the competition in spotting and interpreting the issues and are first to respond with appropriate advice.

Client care

Client care refers to the organisation's ability to understand all their clients and to address their needs. It obviously helps to have a comprehensive database containing information about past purchase history, legal specialisms etc. However, equally important is the building of client relationships and trust at all levels within the business. Client's needs include not only the individual's needs but those of the client's company (assuming they work for an instructing organisation). Needs are categorised as both the client's immediate legal needs and also any longer term needs not yet anticipated.

Organisations must stop thinking of the client in the short-term, case by case but instead look holistically at the client and take a proactive stance. What is the likelihood of repeat instructions? Who else from that organisation instructs on similar matters? What complementary services could be offered? Who else is in the client's supply chain and what services might they need? Is the client happy enough with your organisation to provide references in print and video? Will they speak at events on your behalf? What about prospective clients, what will it take to convert them into clients? In this category differentiators include the speed of responsiveness to clients, the time and care taken to explain the legal process, the after-care service, ongoing communications etc. None of these cost a great deal but all are valuable to the client and are a way in which firms and chambers can differentiate themselves from the competition.

Organisational effectiveness

The third category, organisational effectiveness, refers to the business's ability to operate in a lean and efficient manner. We know that chambers have significantly fewer overheads than law firms and that this is a distinct advantage to them. However, they've also got fewer bodies available to perform the work. Therefore organisations need to look at adapting their operating models to ensure that they are always delivering a high value service to their clients. Strategic partnerships with law firms, accountants or outsourcing businesses can provide significant help to companies looking to efficiently manage their overheads whilst maintaining their flexibility.

Within each of the three areas there are many ways for organisations to differentiate. The best strategies draw on elements from all three categories and reflect the company's personality for consistent branding.

Marketing strategies

A marketing strategy is a process that enables an organisation to focus limited resources on the best ways to increase revenue and achieve a sustainable competitive advantage. It is a collection of high-level rules that direct subsequent marketing activities. For example, if there is a single influencer who touches all your clients and prospects, one of the most sensible strategies will be to build a strong relationship with that influencer so that you become a trusted source of information that they disseminate to the market.

Your marketing strategy is the way you make sure you're getting the maximum impact from your limited marketing budget and time – your marketing plans.

When building a marketing plan, the cornerstone is always the goals of the business. These are the highest-level objectives of the organisation; the mission statement. The next layer of the plan is the overall marketing strategy; the high-level rules that will govern what marketing efforts you focus on. After you've defined your marketing strategy, you will define the marketing mix: plans for product, pricing, place (distribution), people and promotion, otherwise known as the 5Ps. Then the final step is writing a marketing plan, which will describe the specific, detailed marketing activities that you plan on engaging in to achieve the marketing strategies and business goals.

How can legal service providers effectively implement measurable marketing strategies to help them stand out from the crowd and what are the most effective ways of evaluating marketing results and appealing to new and existing clients?

The answer to this million dollar question is this: taking a fresh approach to marketing needs to stem from truly understanding what they currently do (in terms of marketing, service provision and client care) in comparison to what their clients' needs are now and what they are likely to be in the future.

In order to be able to differentiate, you need to understand what you do well and what you don't do well. You will need to determine why people buy your services and, just as important, why they don't. Then, look at the channels by which those services are provided. Do they differ for the different areas of law? If so, which channels are best suited to those areas – joint partnerships with accountants or law firms to provide complete solutions for blue-chip organisations (or indeed on more local levels for regional businesses) or digital marketing and video surgeries for direct access clients?

Successful marketing strategies will flow from the sectors and skills identified, adopting a differentiation approach according to the varying requirements of the target markets.

Once a strategy is operational, how do you know it's successful? Well, that all depends on what you want to measure! There are a whole raft of measurements you can use to track the minutiae of marketing campaigns such as newsletter opens, advert click throughs, website visitors, brochure downloads, social media interaction etc. Each of these are valid metrics and will tell you how the various elements of your campaigns are performing.

However, what ultimately matters is the end result – increased instructions or increased work value. In order to measure this, you'll need to have baseline figures to work from by client, by work type and by legal area. Only then can you see if a concerted campaign into the aviation sector, for example, has produced more instructions than you had previously and if those instructions are 'advice' or 'action' based and what value is attached to each. From this you can calculate your marketing return on investment.

In terms of how to appeal to new and existing clients, the answer is to 'give them what they want… and how and when they want it!' Sounds simple but it's not! You'll need to evaluate exactly how you provide your services and how that provision fits with the needs (both existing and future) of your clients and prospects. The world operates more 24/7 than it ever has – how you do measure up to that? Are you able to provide online services, video consultations and online collaborative working? Are you able to respond quickly to clients on the other side of the globe… or indeed those who work irregular hours just around the corner? How do you know what they want? The answer is marketing research fuelling client service programmes all tied in to the operational aims of the organisation!

Core components of the marketing strategy

Your marketing strategy will explain how your marketing plans will support your organisation's strategic plan and specifically identify the appeal of your products and services.

Elements for you to consider: your organisation uniqueness, legal products and services, positioning within the market; attracting and maintaining your market, cross selling etc.

Positioning statements:-

- Strategic focus on the most important target markets; the market's most important needs; and how your products and services meet those needs.

- State the main competition; how your products and services / counsel are better.

- What is the actual "value" to the client / lay client?

- By using your organisation they can save time/ manage risk / lower costs for their business which in turn enables them to do what?

- The more personal and specific you can make a value statement, the more it will resonate with them.

Pricing strategy:-

- Provide a price breakdown of your products and services and relate your pricing determinants and strategy to your overall marketing strategy. Are you pricing yourself out of certain market sectors?

- Consider things like: what your products and services cost you to produce and sell (cost of barrister + clerk time etc.; solicitor time, fee earner time, secretarial time); what your margins will be; discount policies and strategies; possibility of pricing wars; critical supply and demand factors; how pricing will change over time (especially for legal aid) etc.

- Knowing what your true cost of a case / work / matter type is will help you to determine which areas of work you want to pursue and which you want to avoid, or are prepared to use as a "loss leader".

Promotion strategy:-

- This component of your marketing strategy will answer how you spread the word about your organisation to future clients, and how you will promote your products and services.

- Which channels are best suited to the target market you are focusing on?

- Elements to consider: advertising, public relations, trade shows, events, direct mail, email, internet strategies, social media, seminars, sales literature, expected response rates, promotion costs, name identification, brand loyalty, advertising budgets, incentives; advertising message, theme and vehicles; client communications and so forth.

- It is important to determine the marketable differences in your products and services over your competition.

- You will also need to consider how you manage and track the success of each channel.

Distribution strategy:-

These are some of the questions you should be asking while developing your marketing strategy's distribution:-

- How will you / who will distribute your products and services? What is unique in your distribution strategy compared to the competition? What are your distribution strengths? At first sight this doesn't look relevant for legal service suppliers, however it is very important and can make the difference in winning or losing a client. The key is in understanding how the client wants their services delivered via regular face-to-face contact with you or via more technological approaches.

- Are you offering direct access / public access and if so who is on your panel?

- Are you looking to combine with regional law firms to bid for public contracts? If so whom?

- Are you looking to open offices / work with other chambers or firms in other regions close to your target markets?

- How do you work with clients? Via electronic / web / remote facilities?

Getting to grips with big data and analytics

The primary role of the marketer is to acquire new clients, and retain and grow existing ones. It's a tall order and a job that demands effective use of big data and analytics. Collecting and storing information from various sources, in different formats can be a logistical nightmare. But it's vital. A good customer relationship management (CRM) system is worth its weight in gold for this purpose.

Once the stumbling block of how to store vast quantities of data has been overcome, the next one presents itself… what exactly do you do with it?

Don't allow it to sit dormant. Utilise it to your advantage and allow it to guide objectively based business decisions. Put to good use, analytics can enhance the entire client lifecycle, improve profitability and reduce costs. None of these benefits should be dismissed. They're the basic essentials of any successful business.

But, depending upon whether you were born with a mathematical brain, analytics may not be your strong point. Which is why we've got some well-timed number-crunching advice! While we can't make you a data expert overnight, we can at least introduce you to some of the common data types and metrics.

Ultimately, you're trying to find patterns and gather insight hidden in your vast data repositories to get a 360^0 view of your clients and prospective clients based on 4 main types of data:-

1. Descriptive: self-declared information and demographics.

2. Behavioural: history of enquiries and instructions.

3. Interaction: emails, call records and web activity.

4. Attitudinal: preferences, needs, opinions (generated discovered through survey responses or social media).

Armed with valuable background details such as these allows you to really personalise your marketing, feeding customised offers to a highly targeted (perhaps, even, individualised) audience, instead of simply mass marketing every campaign to everyone in your database.

A popular metric for grading clients is RFM. This acronym stands for recency (when did they last instruct your business?), frequency (how often do they instruct you?) and monetary value (what's their average spend per instruction?). It goes without saying (but we'll say it anyway!) that those with the highest RFM scores are your best clients. There's potentially an upselling opportunity with these clients and any new leads which most closely resemble them are the ones to target.

Of course, an exhaustive list of metrics can be adopted for a whole range of reasons. It could be anything from your client satisfaction ratings (i.e. Net Promoter Score) which helps retain installed base clients to cost-per-acquisition which tells you about the effectiveness of your marketing strategy.

It's generally accepted that over a 5-year period legal businesses could see as many as half of their clients move to competitive offerings. Legal businesses can expect to spend up to 7 times more in terms of cost-per-acquisition of a new client than they would have to spend retaining an existing one. But, businesses which boost client retention rates by as little as 5% could see an increase in profits of between 15% and 30%. This shows us that it's important to understand the value, both existing and potential, of your client base from which you can then devise cost effective programmes to leverage it.

Developing effective marketing plans

Marketing strategy and marketing programmes form your overall marketing plan. These two parts of your marketing plan are closely linked as your marketing programmes will implement your marketing plan's underlying strategies.

It is important to remember that the term "marketing" is defined as the identification of market needs and requirements and the fulfilment of those needs. In effect, marketing is science by which you create awareness, interest, desire and action in your prospect base towards your products and services.

Some marketers' strengths lie in planning. Others, however, prefer the day-to-day tactical activities and like to leave the overriding strategic planning to fate. But this can cause problems for your organisation.

Specifically, you can easily overspend your budget, and sporadic activities may be inconsistent, unsuitable and, therefore, unsuccessful. Also, you can become over reliant on existing business and word-of-mouth recommendations. While this may be enough to keep you ticking over, it means that your competitors are winning lots of new instructions which, with some planned marketing effort, could have been yours.

Planning is vital to lay the marketing foundations for your business and all your marketing activity should be driven by its place in your overall plan.

Don't be daunted by planning. Using a tried-and-tested standardised template will make the planning process easier. Work through each element below in turn and you have your marketing plan for the next few months. It is customary to plan for 3 months in advance, to be reviewed and refined quarterly. A marketing plan isn't static – it should be modified on an ongoing basis depending on what works and what doesn't and how the market is evolving.

Item 1: Internal audit

With this in mind, the first item in your template should be an audit of historical marketing activities. What methods have you used to promote your chambers, how much did you spend and what results did you gain? Ditch the time wasters and retain the winners.

Item 2: Wider audit

Widen your audit to identify and analyse your main competitors. Compare your service offering to theirs. If you're better, tell people why you're special or different. If you're worse, do something about it!

Item 3: Objective setting

Now that you know your positioning, decide where you want to be. This is where you set your SMART objectives for the next 12 months. Your overriding goal comes first (i.e. increase turnover from £X to £Y with X% from existing clients and Y% from new instructions) then your smaller objectives which will help you to achieve it (i.e. exhibit at X industry events). Remember that they must be SMART which means specific, measurable, achievable, realistic and timed.

Item 4: Market research

Research your target market. What are their needs and how can you address them? Where do they congregate (i.e. online communities, events, legal publications) and how can you engage in conversation with them there?

Item 5: Activity planning

Finally, produce a shortlist of your chosen marketing activities and best channels. This is the tactical part of your plan and will encompass everything ranging from advertising and networking to direct mail and PR.

In all likelihood, your plan will comprise a combination of descriptive text and statistical data in table-like format. It's useful if you can log your activities and spends so that you can track actual against budgeted costs. That way, you know which tasks are completed and how much money you have left to spend from your marketing budget.

Marketing your services internationally

Many companies operate internationally. Although marketing overseas bears many similarities to marketing domestically, regional differences prevent the use of a 'one-size-fits-all' approach to your marketing planning process.

Variations in values, customs, languages and other social or economic factors should be acknowledged. Also, an effective overseas marketing plan should comprise more than just face-to-face visits once or twice a year. While it's essential to visit in person, such limited contact isn't enough to build firm relationships and grow a global brand.

People the world over demand legal services at some point in their personal or professional lives. So, to secure your stake in other lucrative markets overseas, you need a dedicated marketing plan to target your clients and prospective clients with a scheduled series of marketing communications and promotional activities.

Of course, some marketers would argue that a standardised approach will suffice but proponents of standardisation fail to account for important country-specific differences. For example, the existence of advertising restrictions, media availability, technology usage etc. All of which dictate the types of marketing mix components which are relevant to the country's local culture and tastes. The best strategy is one of adaptation.

As with a traditional marketing plan, the components of your marketing mix can be equally diverse in order to maximise the touch-points with your stakeholder groups.

Overseas visits

Depending on the location of your international site(s), your visit in terms of travel expenses alone could be extremely costly. So make your trip worthwhile. Your regular customers and hottest prospects will only know about your visit if you tell them about it beforehand.

Write to them, either by email or post (depending on their preferences), to advise of your imminent arrival on their home territory. Devise a meeting rota and invite them to meet with you either at your or their office (where practicable).

Of course, it's impossible to meet up with everyone on a one-to-one basis. There are only 24 hours in a day and some of those must be spent sleeping! Therefore, would a party or other informal gathering be appropriate too? Source local suppliers for venues (if there isn't sufficient room in your offices), catering and entertainment, then invite people along. Spread your social butterfly wings and mingle. Afterwards, follow up with further emails or letters and start converting those leads.

<u>Systematic communications</u>

If you only visit once a year, don't abandon your clientele for the remaining 11 months. If you forget about them, they'll forget about you. Maintain regular communications. Keep them informed about the hot topics within their country; what's happening in your chambers; legal and regulatory changes or developments. By staying at the forefront of their minds, you're increasing your chances of acquiring new or repeat business.

Work through the 7Ps (product, price, promotion, place, physical evidence, people and process) of service marketing to compile your marketing mix. Be sensitive to the unique characteristics of your population but inventive too, in order to stand out from the crowd.

Communicating value

Is it the role of lawyers to communicate the changes affecting the justice system and their own value to clients / consumers and if so, how do they go about it?

The answer is, undoubtedly yes, it is the role of legal service providers (not necessarily individual lawyers) to communicate changes in the justice system to their clients and the wider public and also to communicate their own value.

Any organisation that takes the lead in an evolving market and can communicate clear and concise value statements will have a competitive advantage over its rivals. It is perceived as a "thought leader" and "trusted source of information". That perception builds reputation which in turn leads to increased instructions. The same applies in the legal market, however, it is not a simple task.

By taking the lead, innovative organisations can communicate changes before anyone else. They can explain the changes in relation to the clients and furthermore they can illustrate their own "value" by doing so.

They need to communicate changes in a manner that the clients can fully understand.

- How does the change impact on the client (or lay client)?

- What do they need to be aware of?

- How do they need to act differently to remain compliant with the law?

- What benefit is there to the client in buying the legal service from us?

The value of the organisation is not simply in dealing with the aftermath of events, but instead in understanding the client's needs and pre-empting any potentially damaging situations. If you segment the market correctly, the process of building relationships and communicating value becomes easier.

For organisations dealing with the general public, it's much more difficult.

There is still a need to communicate changes in a manner that the clients can fully understand. However, communicating with the public requires the ability to talk in plain English and it requires a large financial investment. It also requires a multi-channel approach (advertising, TV, radio, direct mail, face-to-face, social etc.) and, with it, substantial investment.

However, smaller organisations can use social media, comparison sites and joint marketing with other companies to create differentiation and communicate their value. They just need to be a little more creative in communicating their value propositions!

Conclusion

The main takeaways from this chapter are:-

1. Operational implementation strategies must feed into the corporate strategy otherwise they will fail.

2. If the strategic goals of the organisation are not communicated to everyone in the organisation, the plan will fail.

3. If the members of the organisation don't buy into the strategic goals, the business will fail.

4. Using SWOT analysis gives you insights into your business and enables you to make the necessary adjustments for success.

5. B2B and B2C marketing is very different, you will need to select the right methods for your business.

6. There are many different business models available to lawyers. Understanding your goals and clients will enable you to select the correct operational model to use.

7. Differentiation is the key to competitive advantage.

8. There are a number of ways to differentiate within three broad strategies: service innovation, client care and organisational effectiveness.

9. A marketing strategy is a process that enables an organisation to focus limited resources on the best ways to increase revenue and achieve a sustainable competitive advantage.

10. Core components of a marketing strategy include price, product, promotion, people and distribution.

11. Elements to consider in your strategy include: your organisation uniqueness, legal products and services, positioning within the market, attracting and maintaining your market, cross selling etc.

12. Good planning and communication are essential.

CHAPTER TWO
THE IMPORTANCE OF
BRANDING IN LAW

Used to give products and services a unique identity or personality, a brand enables organisations to differentiate themselves from the competition. An additional benefit is that the consumers may become brand loyal and thus repeat purchasers.

A brand is not simply a name, nor is it just a logo, although that's an important part of it. A brand is the culmination of the organisation's values and aspirations. Sounds rather lofty, but in order to understand how to create and use a brand properly, you need to appreciate what a brand actually is and how it works.

Branding is becoming increasingly important within the legal services sector. You might not want to hear this but branding's not an overnight fix. Branding's a long-term process but one that's worth the effort because the benefits of a strong brand identity are wide-reaching. The advantages range from encouraging client loyalty, shortening decision making processes, enabling the positioning of higher pricing and increasing the value of your business. Let's explain further.

Clients who know and recognise a brand (by this we mean that they understand exactly what they will get should they choose that brand in terms of client service, value and sometimes even kudos) do not have to go through a lengthy decision making process. They are more likely to purchase services with this perceived trusted brand rather than 'risk' using a lesser known alternative. This is particularly the case when the stakes for the client are higher. They are also more likely to instruct your organisation on areas of law that they haven't done previously.

Where customer loyalty's concerned, obviously the client experience must have been exceptional. As we know, the best way to increase profits is to leverage from existing clients, so where we can build a strong and trusted brand we can retain clients at a fraction of the cost of acquiring new ones.

A strong and trusted brand also permits us to charge more for services, as clients perceive brands as deserving a higher value than homogenous services. This is particularly useful for high-street practices where they are having to compete against many other firms offering similar services for the same clients.

Finally, a brand can have a financial value and can be viewed as an asset. This is particularly useful when looking for external investment in the organisation.

Large firms are putting are putting enormous amounts of money into branding campaigns designed to build awareness, trust and customer loyalty as well as to communicate the values of the organisation. But if you've not got their budget, there are many brand building activities you can do to benefit your organisation.

In this chapter, read about:-

- Developing a brand strategy

- Internal marketing

Developing a brand strategy

There are three main types of brand strategy. You will probably be best served by combining all three.

Corporate branding – this is where the organisation uses its own name for all products and services. Examples include IBM, Nike and Marks & Spencer. Using a top level brand in this way is a cost-effective way to build brand recognition and a 'global' image. It uses less design expense as it tends to be logo driven. However, for it to be successful the brand values must be communicated clearly. The potential danger of relying on just corporate branding is that one failure in terms of service can severely damage the brand reputation.

Family branding – for lawyers this would be the practice areas. It involves using a secondary brand image and name for the specific practice areas. It leverages from the main corporate brand but then applies that to the relevant sectors. It enables those sectors to carry specific messages that will resonate with potential clients, and so it needs to be applied with care, particularly if you are considering cross-selling services at a later date.

Individual branding – in the consumer market this is the level of branding that we are most familiar with; Kit Kat, Coke etc. In law, it relates to the individual lawyer (more commonly barrister) who has excelled in a particular field of expertise. This is one of the reasons that directory rankings are hugely important as they provide an independent view of who is the 'best' in any given area.

Using a mixture of the branding approaches enables you to promote your services to individuals and companies simultaneously to best effect.

<u>Understanding your brand – what does it represent?</u>

Identifying what your brand stands for can be a complex business. What are the company values your brand represents (hopefully those of trust, integrity and knowledge)? What kind of image is best associated with those words? What colours will provide an accurate reflection of your strengths and markets (there are certain colours that are associated with specific words – it's a whole psychological / sociological area of its own, for example, blue represents calm, green environmental, orange communication etc.)? It's no wonder that companies often turn to brand agencies to help them with this. However, if you don't have that kind of money, you can do it yourself – but be warned it takes a lot of time and effort.

You'll need to understand what your brand position is at the moment. You'll need to do this by surveying the market – what do clients, former clients and prospective clients think about your business? Why do they instruct you and how do you compare with the competition? What key words do they associate with their experiences? From here you should be able to pull common threads and develop those into a more cohesive branding value statement. From that you can look at symbols and colours associated with those words and phrases (as well as any logo you may already have – there's no point in throwing everything away just to be trendy).

Once you have your brand statements, your logo and your colour board (be aware that logos will need to be printed in many formats – therefore you will need full colour, black and white and reduced colour or single pallet variants of your logo capable of being reproduced in all sizes from website to full scale A1 or beyond. We cover logo design in more detail later).

You may be tempted into a strap-line such as 'Good with …' in the case of the Co-op (later changed to 'Here for you for life'. However, you must consider all the scenarios in which this line may be used. Clearly they were on to something with food and banking (Good with Food, Good with Money) but it all went a bit pear-shaped when it came to the funeral services! You also need to consider translating any strap-lines into other languages for international markets or clients. Again, you really need to be careful here. The Pepsi slogan 'Come alive with the Pepsi Generation' suffered somewhat in translation in Taiwan as it became 'Pepsi will bring your ancestors back from the dead'!

How to communicate a brand

Now you have your brand and image propositions sorted, you will need to communicate your brand. This is done via everything you, your staff and / or members do. There is no underestimating the power of brands and the damage that people can inadvertently do to them. Therefore everyone in the organisation must understand the brand, understand the values and buy into them fully.

You will need to issue everyone with brand guidelines, so that they know exactly what is expected of them (this is easier said than done, particularly within barristers' chambers where some individuals battle against a corporate identity).

Here is a flavour of what should be included in your brand guidelines to ensure that the brand is communicated consistently throughout your business:-

- Telephone protocol – how do you want people to answer the phone, usually it would flow along the lines of 'good morning /afternoon, XYZ Company, ABC speaking, how can I help you?'

- Email addresses and signatures – clear concise and with the relevant social media links and logos.

- Stationery – fonts, logos, colours, VAT details – use of Word document templates for all staff / members.

- Business cards – need to follow the format of your email signatures.

- Signage – an array of sizes and uses with correct placement and type of logo.

- Sales literature – brochures, services sheets, case studies, proposals – again these need to have pre-determined and correct placements of logos.

- Advertising – supply examples of the types of advertisements and the style of font, sentiment, contact details and logo placement.

- Exhibition and display material – consider what you are using it for and how it will carry the details clearly.

- PowerPoint presentations – create templates with consistent branding so that anyone can just add their content. Consider having a 'corporate' slide set that details the headline figures / propositions of your whole organisation. The advantages here are consistency of corporate information without limiting the creativity of the individual presentation.

- Corporate clothing and gifts – these need to be in keeping with the values of your brand as well as carrying the corporate colour and logo.

- Recruitment advertising – like normal advertising, this needs to be clear and concise.

- Mailings – consider the many different types of formats and how the brand can be represented consistently across all formats.

- Internal staff communications – the branding must be consistent at all times, including in internal communications.

- Press releases – create a 'boilerplate' for your business. This is a standard paragraph of text that clearly and concisely explains what you do, for whom and where. The boilerplate fits into the bottom of any press release so that editors may pull information from there as required.

Email plays an increasingly important role in how we work and how we communicate with clients and prospects. It's therefore important to look at how we use email to communicate and how we can use this tool for best effect.

In the business world, email is the primary tool used for communication. In a law firm or clerks' room comprising 10 clerks / fee earners, if each one sends an average of 30 emails, that's 300 emails per day. And that's a conservative estimate.

A personalised email from a known, trusted source has an open rate of 90% and higher. If your emails contain subtle marketing messages, that's a lot of people you're reaching with important information on offers, events or news, simply and for free.

This is why you need to pay attention to your email signature.

The space at the foot of your email is called your email signature. Just as with a postal letter, this should always at least contain your name, position, company and contact details. However, you can use this area to promote yourself and your organisation without being overly salesy.

The following will give you some ideas on how to optimise your email signature to take advantage of this passive form of marketing and start securing potential new business leads:-

Basics with a bonus – We've already mentioned that your emails should feature your basic personal details, much as they would appear on your business card. Expand this to show your full contact information, including postal address, with links to social media profiles.

Integrated marketing promotions – If you're running a campaign to promote your organisation's services or forthcoming events, tie in to your email signature for consistent messaging across all marketing channels for greater impact.

Shout about your achievements – Have you won any industry awards? Featured in directories? Are you supporting a charity? Do you belong to any legal panels or undertake pro bono work? Have any members / fee earners received special recognition for outstanding service? Have you won any landmark cases? Be loud and proud by telling others all about it in your email signature.

Imagery and colours – Lines of continuous black text are boring and likely to be missed by your recipients. Think about branding. Use your corporate colours and company logo in your email signature so that it stands out from the main body content. Remember to keep the graphic size small though and include a description in the file properties to stop it getting held up by spam filters.

If you're feeling adventurous, create a set of artwork graphics using images and copy to depict your message more visually. You may need to play around with pixel dimensions to get the size right. Be aware that some email systems or company servers automatically block and strip images, so use a mix of words and artwork to get your message across, and add an alt-text (alternative text) tag which your reader will see when the image can't be rendered.

Set up several dynamic email signatures.

Depending upon the sophistication of your email system, you may be able to set up several email signatures for different purposes and domain names. As with other forms of marketing, this enables you to segment and target your market with tailored, relevant messages.

As well as communicating via email, PowerPoints and Slide Shares are becoming increasingly popular tools of brand communication, particularly as they can be uploaded to social media and websites so that clients can download them on demand. With that in mind, you need to ensure that your presentations adhere to the brand guidelines and deliver the messages in a consistent manner.

For presentations intended primarily for download you may like to include video or audio sequences to make it a little more interesting and also hyperlinks to where the readers may find further information. Calls to action should be used on the last slide to encourage people to contact you directly should they have a requirement for your services.

Internal marketing

Internal marketing is inward-facing marketing. Its goal is to align every aspect of a company's internal operations so that it operates in a co-ordinated, standardised way. By doing so, clients experience a consistent level of service. You've spent a great deal of time and effort in establishing a leading brand, you need to ensure that your people are a reflection of those brand values. The best way to do this is with a satisfied, motivated workforce tuned in to the importance of client centricity – i.e. putting your clients at the centre of your philosophy – as they will provide value to your clients at every touchpoint.

The issue lies in most legal service providers' lack of expertise in internal marketing; if they do it at all. We find the responsibility usually lies with HR; professionals without marketing skills. The real power of internal marketing is to convince your staff to become protectors of your brand; not just tell them occasional firm / chambers news which tends to be the general way of things.

The benefits of internal marketing include:-

1. Client-oriented workforce: with optimum client service levels, keep your client base for the long term and ease the pressure on your new business initiatives.

2. Improved staff retention: happy employees stay longer so you save money on recruitment and training costs.

3. Enhanced external business relationships: for stronger link building with all your stakeholders.

4. Increased compliance with standards and protocols: supporting your client service or change initiatives and strengthening your brand reputation.

5. Empowered decision making: with the responsibility to act within certain guidelines, your staff will make valuable contributions to support your decision-making processes.

6. Greater sense of teamwork and higher morale: job satisfaction leads to better dispositions at work and less conflict so that everyone works as a team and productivity increases too. For you, that's profit!

As a legal service provider, your staff perform a pivotal role in your organisation. Happy, motivated, skilled workers provide good customer service. That means satisfied clients who will return to your firm / set time and time again to bring repeat business. The opposite – unhappy, demotivated, untrained workers – are likely to underperform. That means dissatisfied clients who will seek better service from another supplier.

Obviously, the first scenario is what you're aiming to achieve in your quest for success. To ensure your employees serve your clients with enthusiasm and expertise, you need to implement internal marketing programmes focused on training and motivating staff.

There are some simple strategies for internal marketing:-

Communications: Monthly newsletters, meetings or briefings maintain a clear line of communication between all of your organisation's employees and members. These should include information on all practice areas so that everyone has an understanding of what's going on and how they can cross-sell services into their own clients.

Appraisals and training: Spot shortfalls in knowledge or additional skills requirements by routine appraisals then source appropriate training courses or mentoring schemes to bridge the gap. The lawyers in your organisation should be doing this as part of their continued professional development obligations, but other staff in your set should do the same. That way, everyone in the organisation is working to improve their own situation and education.

Rewards and recognition: It's good to know that hard work doesn't go unnoticed. Make it your mission to spot your staff's efforts. Acknowledge in as formal or informal means as you choose. This could take the form of a monetary reward or simple 'well done'.

Responsibility and promotion: Assign additional responsibilities to those who've identified the desire and demonstrated the capability to handle a heavier workload. It shows how much you believe in them. Similarly, offering staff the chance for career advancement gives them an incentive to always perform at their best in their search for the next step on the proverbial career ladder.

Earn people-focused accreditation: By securing widely known awards such as Investors in People and Best Companies, you're showing your staff and the world at large how much you care about your workforce. Even if you don't at first attain the standard you were hoping for, the accreditation programmes will provide you with a clear roadmap for change for better results next time round.

So, start taking internal marketing more seriously and you'll soon be wowing your clients with genuine customer care and cementing your brand as the leader in that field.

Conclusion

The main takeaways from this chapter are:-

1. A brand is not simply a name, nor is it a logo. A brand is the culmination of the organisation's values and aspirations.

2. If used correctly a brand can inspire staunch customer loyalty.

3. There are three main types of brand strategy (corporate, family and individual). You will probably be best served by combining all three.

4. The best place to start is to understand your current brand value using research into prospective clients and established clients.

5. Brand guidelines are essential for everyone in the business to be 'on message'.

6. Internal marketing is essential for communicating the brand values and ensuring a client-centric organisation.

CHAPTER THREE
ENSURING SUCCESSFUL
COMMUNICATIONS

Marketing is all about establishing then maintaining relationships. If you're thinking this only applies to business-to-consumer (B2C) marketing, you're wrong. Even if you operate in a strictly business-to-business (B2B) environment, it's the people behind the companies you're reaching out to.

For any relationship to be successful, communication's essential. Regular communication.

Without getting bogged down by theory, because that's not what this book is about, from a marketing perspective, communication falls under the promotion element of the marketing mix's four Ps. The other three being price, place and product. When marketing services, of course, the extended marketing mix applies, whose seven Ps include the additional categories of people, processes and physical evidence.

Anyway, now that we know where communication fits into the complex jigsaw of marketing, just how do we set about doing it? There's no simple answer to this million-dollar question because, as people, we're all different. While one person converses largely by email, another's a fan of hard copy letters. While one person's on the lookout for white paper resources to cement their learning in a particular area, another's sourcing instant visual gratification in videos for an overview of a specific subject.

Your marketing communications plan should be reasonably broad in order to be effective. Relying solely on a single communication vehicle is not likely to produce good results. The reality, then, is that marketers have to cater for all preferences. By doing so, you can reach out effectively to everyone within your target audience by providing the information they desire, in the format they want, on the platform they spend their time.

The challenge is this: the content and writing style vary drastically. Unfortunately there's no single approach fits all. Here we'll tackle each of the main methods of communication, including:-

- Email marketing

- Direct mail

- Newsletters

- White papers

- Videos

It's worth mentioning here that at the core of your campaign plans should be the needs of your client or prospect, not self-centredness. Campaign recipients don't want to be told all about you as and when you feel like telling them. They want to know how you're going to help them with their problems at a time and place convenient to them. Remember this always.

Listen to your clients to find out about their concerns. This may be from phone conversations, in-person meetings, social network discussions, blog commentaries, surveys or interviews. Ask what's keeping them up at night and their top challenges for the next calendar year. These are great sources of information. Plan content for your campaigns by addressing these issues. Hear the voice of your client or prospect when writing content and you can't go far wrong.

So, let's get you started…

Email marketing

Email communications are cheap, fast, far-reaching and measurable (especially if you use an emailer system), making it one of the most widely used digital marketing tactics.

But, everyone's in on the act. It's estimated that approximately 120 billion business emails are sent every day (and growing!). That's a busy inbox. We receive more and more emails each day and have ever-diminishing time in which to read them. Click-through rates vary industry to industry, customer to prospect, opt-in to purchased database. An oft-quoted baseline is 15%.

Here's how to get your emails noticed amongst the masses:-

Use a personal from address

This is all about your company brand on an individual relationship level. Even if recipients know your law firm, however, they're likely to ignore info@ email addresses. Emails from personal email addresses stand a much greater chance of being opened.

Craft your subject line

Once you've carefully crafted the pitch-perfect email, do you give as much consideration to your subject line? 80% of your email's success is attributed to the subject line. Despite their brevity, writing email subject lines for maximum audience engagement is no small task. To win over your recipients from the outset:-

- Use "how to" titles which solve popular industry issues – a law firm or individual facing similar problems will be interested straightaway

- Incorporate the words "infographics", "videos", "photos" and "webinars" – these descriptors are proven to increase engagement

- Embed numbers – such as "top 5 reasons" or "3 ways to" – it gives the impression of being easily digestible

- Ask an intriguing question – touch a chord and you've got your reader hooked

- Avoid caps lock – if you use capitals for whole words and sentences, your readers will imagine you're shouting at them

- Keep away from exclamation marks too – for the same reason

- Don't use spam words – filters are searching for words such as "trial offer", "guaranteed", "call now" and many, many more of these over-used marketing terms

- Be honest – make false claims or promises and you'll lose the trust of your subscribers so ensure the sentiment of your subject line is legitimate

- Be consistent – if you send regular communications, make it easy for your readers to spot new emails and find old ones which they may wish to re-visit

- Get straight to the point – fire your biggest gun first by placing the most important words early in your subject line

- Take your time – considering the power of your subject line, don't rush it or write as an after-thought to the campaign copywriting process

- Proof read – once drafted, proof it; a typo or confused message looks sloppy and will not impress readers

- Test it – shorter subject lines tend to perform better but every email system and mobile device allows for different character lengths so test and see what works best

- Think about length – following on from the above, run out of characters and part of your headline (perhaps the crucial part!) will be lost

- Be light-hearted – this isn't always possible but, where the subject matter permits, introduce a spot of humour; lightening the mood can help get recipients on your side

Utilise the preview header space

Your preview gives a sneak peek into your email. From there, recipients can decide if they think what you're offering is personal and meaningful. It's essential that your first sentence is enticing, to the point and matches your subject line.

Address recipients by their first name

Make emails personal. Use your recipient's first name and utilise the words "you" and "your" throughout. It's all about them, remember?

Jump to the point

Email readers have short attention spans so skip long introductions and backgrounds or they'll read no further than your opening sentences. State everything clearly, with minimal words. The KISS (keep it simple, stupid) acronym applies.

Talk about them, not you!

In the middle section of your email, include a few short sentences setting out exactly how you can solve their problems or make their professional life easier. Bullet points are quick to scan and read, so use bulleted lists where possible.

Focus on benefits not features

Where a pitch is presented, set out the benefits. Imagine you're them for a moment. Are they truly benefits and would you act on the email if your roles were reversed?

Write as you talk

If your language is too formal or contains technical lingo, reading's a heavier slog and it can be misunderstood. Conversational English wins hands down every time.

Embed URLs

In your signature or footer section, incorporate hyperlinks to your website, blog or portfolio. Readers should be able to find out more about you in one click.

Add value and call your recipients to action

Your email needs a call to action that adds value, for example, accessing a free demonstration or viewing some statistics to support your argument. Make it clear what they should do next to maintain conversation. If no action or reply is sought, say it. It'll be music to their ears!

Use e-cards when appropriate

If you're sending e-cards with, for example, Christmas greetings, and you're already using an emailer system, then it's a simple process of setting up a new template, perhaps taking out the standard disclaimer notices so that it doesn't detract from the card's messaging and scheduling as appropriate in the run up to the festive holidays.

If you don't use an emailer system, you could instead use a dedicated e-card website. Some of these sites are free but most are chargeable so make sure that you check the associated costs and subscription information, as you may end up signing up for months when you only need to use it on a one-off basis. You can get creative with e-cards, utilising a mix of music, sound and moving images to really invoke the spirit of the season.

Test and analyse

Test different content, times, days, subject lines etc. and see what works best for your audience. If you're able to, look at campaign results to identify patterns for success. If something works, it's more of the same. It something fails, it's back to the drawing board.

<u>Maximise your content</u>

Pick out the emails related to a larger topic umbrella, connect together like a puzzle and revise accordingly so the content flows smoothly and you've got a lengthier content piece suitable for another channel and audience. This is called re-purposing.

Another way to re-purpose content is to simply share them again. To re-share, include an "ICYMI" (in case you missed it) tag. This tells your current audience that they're seeing something they've already read, and informs your new audience that this is an important piece of content they've previously missed.

Email is a great relationship building tool for brands and their customers, but it's important to remember that a good relationship is about listening as well as talking. By listening to customers and taking the time to understand who they are and what they like, law firms can deliver emails at the correct frequency, optimised for the right device, which contain the right type of content for the recipient. The more advanced the industry gets, the more important it becomes to listen and respond in as close to real-time as possible.

Direct mail

Direct mail is the delivery of advertising material by post. Sadly, direct mail hasn't earned its nickname, junk mail, for nothing. Overused, badly written and untargeted communications have given direct mail a bad reputation. Not without good reason in many instances.

Furthermore, it's not cheap. Consider for a moment the cost of postage alone. At the time of going to print, Royal Mail costs are 65p first class or 56p second class for an A5-size letter, increasing to 98p first class or 76p second class for an A4-size letter. Then there's the cost to purchase envelopes, buy letter-headed paper and produce supporting collateral (flyers, brochures, newsletters etc.) or other attachments (promotional giveaways).

However, do it right and direct mail gives you the power to communicate 1-to-1 with your clients and prospects, hitting large volumes of contacts with personalised messages simultaneously. Average response rates sit between 1.1% and 4.4% so the return on investment can be substantial.

Let's calculate a moment. If you mail 100 clients, it costs circa. £200 for the mailer including postage, you achieve 3% response rate, all of these convert to orders and your average order value is £150. That's £250 profit or 125% ROI.

To make direct mail a staple in your marketing plan, follow these guidelines:-

Grow and cleanse your database

Take some time to tidy up your list. This relates to every type of communication but none more so than direct mail where potential wastage costs are highest. It's mundane but critical preparation.

Keeping your list tidy requires regular housekeeping because people and companies move address, close up shop, get married or divorced and change their name, branch out into other areas of business and die. The worst thing you can do is mail someone who's just passed away. Your insensitivity will not be appreciated by those grieving.

It may be more convenient to buy a list but it's better to send a newsletter to 200 interested readers than 2000 disinterested ones. The "opt in" approach is by far the most effective method.

Buy only from reputable suppliers

If building your own list is impossible due to time constraints then ensure you research suppliers, and look for those who can provide mailing lists for your niche market and are well known. Buying dirty lists full of false leads and out-of-date data will waste money and cause more harm than good.

Personalise your heart out

If your list allows, personalise your direct mail, not only in terms of addressee information but also in tailored messaging. After all, being addressed as "Mr Smith" is preferable to "Sir / Madam", and recipients won't want to hear about all your service offerings, just the ones relevant to their area of business or personal circumstances. Leveraging information on their purchasing behaviour and preferences allows you to segment closely, customise content and drive sales.

Segment and target your audience

Mailing everyone on your list will drain your budget with little to show for it. Instead, segment your audience according to your message, for example postcode areas, size, job role and area specialisms. This is particularly prevalent if follow-up activity (i.e. phone calls) is planned, otherwise later tasks will become unmanageable. Choose quality over quantity every time.

Set up a landing page on your website

Create a dedicated landing page and provide recipients with a campaign-specific, easy-to-type (as you can't copy and paste from printed collateral) URL or embed scannable QR codes so that those with online preferences can switch to the web. Your tailored landing page should further reinforce your message.

Carefully craft your message

It's a human being reading your letter so adopt a more casual tone. Use "you" and "your" as much as possible; break up text with questions, headings, subheadings and bullet points; focus predominantly on benefits; support with client testimonials, facts and figures; and utilise the postscript.

Let your creative streak run wild with enclosures

Consider enclosures for added weight and interest. The first goal is to get your envelopes opened. If the enclosure is lumpy, you'll achieve higher open rates out of sheer curiosity.

Open with a bang

Don't build up excitement towards your value proposition, open with it. Get the reader's attention from the word go and they're more likely to read on. Your value proposition is essentially your promise of a solution to a problem or delivery of a host of benefits to make your reader's life easier. It explains why they should send business your way instead of to your competitors.

Use a call to action

Include a specific call to action so that, when your copywriting has worked its magic, your recipients know what to do next. This could be to ring your new business team, come to your next event, subscribe to your email newsletters etc.

Get the timing right

It may be a cliché, but there are seasonal trends in law. Matrimonial cases in September and January, insolvency in April, conveyancing in the spring etc. Consider the time of year when planning the theme and content. Also, schedule your direct mail door mat hits to coincide with other promotional efforts (that's integrated marketing to you and me!) for maximum impact.

Plan, write and edit

For the actual copywriting process itself, divide your time into three stages. First, plot your ideas. Second, write the first draft. Third, edit meticulously. Be convincing with your copywriting and success is guaranteed.

Look great on paper

Strong design is absolutely essential for direct mail marketing. Be bold and inventive. You may need to hire a graphic designer and instruct a printing company to help you out. A striking-looking, professionally printed design is much preferable to chaotic, colour-streaked materials. Aesthetics aren't everything – your copywriting plays a major role – but your recipients will notice the difference.

Use handwritten envelopes with stamps

Your recipients can spot mass-mailed communications from a mile away. The best thing you can do to make it seem like your envelope's been sent from a person rather than a machine is to hand write addresses. If this simply isn't feasible, due to the volume, then use a handwriting-style font. Then complete the look with a stamp rather than whizzing everything through your franking machine. Getting your envelope opened is your first priority so it's worth the effort.

Test the water first

Of the varying methods of communication, direct mail is by far the most expensive. Don't spend your marketing budget on one full-blown campaign. Test a small segment then tweak (if necessary) and send to a larger group once you've determined your rate of return.

Send seasonal cards

The obvious example here is Christmas cards which are a perfect way of showing your clients that you're thinking of them. There are many options: humorous; traditional; contemporary; non-denominational; uniquely designed; pre-printed greetings, signature and envelopes; off-the shelf; and charity.

Whichever you choose, branding is vital so that recipients instantly recognise the sender. There's no point spending huge sums of money on all-singing, all-dancing cards if the reader doesn't know who it's from. But keep it subtle.

Newsletters

Newsletters are another popular communication medium. Whether electronic or print, the production of newsletters is a heavy time investment. The multi-page format demands several articles set out in an aesthetically pleasing and easy-to-read way, incorporating artwork and following your corporate brand guidelines. There can be a significant cost investment too, not only in relation to the copywriting and graphic design input, but also print costs.

With so much at stake, therefore, you need to make sure your newsletters are in good shape. Here's how to make your newsletters work harder for you:-

Choose your format

A well-written, nicely printed newsletter is a beautiful piece of marketing collateral for use in direct mail campaigns or to distribute at events. The problem is that hard copy newsletters can be pricey and you get no useful statistics from which to measure who's read it and acted upon it.

Conversely, electronic newsletters are a mere fraction of the cost, can be set up without assistance from third parties and come with supporting numerical information such as open rates, click through rates, forward rates, deliveries, bounces and unsubscribes (plus more) which allows you to benchmark and continually improve campaigns.

Utilising both formats in tandem is the best approach.

Plan, plan, plan

Decide on the frequency of your newsletters, overall message, then create a schedule for the coming months. This may sound daunting but all you actually need is a 3-column table setting out the date, topic and call to action. For example, your first line entry may be a summer newsletter covering financial investment with the CTA as a click through to a special web page which gives comprehensive details on sound investment advice.

Generate killer content

Write copy relevant to your intended audience. This may be sharing expertise, giving guidance, offering discounts, holding contests, and presenting facts and testimonials. Providing articles of value bolsters your stature as an authority in your field. Your sales pitches have no place here. You shouldn't actually need to use your newsletters as a selling platform anyway. If your content's good enough, you'll demonstrate your knowledge and automatically sell yourself.

Take inspiration from newspaper formatting

Years and years of reading newspapers has taught us to scan for headlines, sub headings, bullet point text, eye-catching imagery and captions. Draw inspiration from this. Write punchy headlines, make your lead story interesting, adopt multi-column formats with broken-up text, and use colour and pictures liberally with captions where appropriate.

Varying font types is a good idea too. However, don't go completely overboard or you'll cause distraction. We recommend no more than three font types overall.

Re-purpose, re-use and re-send

Don't let your hard work go unnoticed. Re-purpose content soundbites for social media to target non-newsletter recipients. Also re-send electronic newsletters to non-openers on a different day, at a different time and perhaps with a different subject line. You might just strike lucky second (or third) time round.

Define your newsletter's regularity

As a minimum, we suggest quarterly newsletters with additional one-off editions for special events. Ideally, commit to monthly newsletters so that recipients are constantly reminded that you're there waiting to take their cases when the time's right.

Be loyal to your brand

Keep your collateral consistent. They may have their own nuances but avoid drastic changes. Use your logo and corporate colour palette. You want your readers to recognise your practice.

Track and report

Monitor the success (or otherwise) of your campaigns. Analyse which work best and try to understand why, then refine future newsletters with this in mind. With printed newsletters, this is a challenge. You're reliant on verbal or written feedback from recipients. With electronic newsletters, it's a straightforward matter of accessing your accompanying statistical reports.

Make it easy for people to subscribe

Creating a sign up function on your website or email footer is a nice touch. Capture basic contact details only at this stage so that you don't put people off at the first hurdle by requesting too much personal data. A name and email (or postal) address will suffice.

White papers

White papers are the ultimate form of content marketing. B2B buyers consistently rank white papers as the most important content type that influences their purchase decisions. They're used for many purposes, from generating sales leads to presenting important business cases. Primarily, though, law firms and barristers' chambers publish white papers to establish themselves as thought leaders in their specialist fields.

Demonstrating your expertise through the distribution of insightful white paper collateral sends a clear signal to your clients and soon-to-be clients that it's your practice, rather than another, whom they should instruct for these chosen legal areas.

To create great white papers, you need to:-

Choose hot industry topics

If there's a pressing issue, show readers how to overcome it. The best white papers provide answers to the questions your readers typically ask. So, what pains does your audience experience and which of these problems can you help them to solve? Your aim is to address one significant issue only to really focus your argument.

Present logical arguments with bite-size snippets as takeaways

Well-researched, perfectly written content will keep your readers engaged from beginning to end. Clearly communicate the most important aspects in strategically placed summary sections for those time-starved skim readers.

Keep it informal

Don't worry about grammatical and syntax rules such as incomplete sentences or non-standard punctuation. Speaking in your reader's language is more important than adhering rigidly to the rule book. Just because it's a more serious piece of marketing material, doesn't mean it has to be dull.

Landscape versus portrait orientation

If you intend to print and circulate hard copies of your white paper, use portrait format. If your white paper is destined for online-only usage, consider landscape for optimal use of web-screen space on computers, laptops and tablets. However, as readers expect landscape set-up pretty much universally these days, you may prefer to adhere to tradition.

Enlist a graphic designer

The layout of your white paper deserves as much consideration as the content. If it's word perfect but everything's cluttered together on a badly designed PDF, your content won't get read. Pay attention to design details such as typography, spacing, images and other formatting. It may sound trivial but it makes the world of difference.

Involve influencers

If you've got reference sites, utilise them to back up your claims. It's an ego boost for your practice and reinforces your credentials. Facts, figures and quotes from reliable sources add proof to your argument. Gather your evidence and use it wisely.

Re-use time and time again

Larger content pieces such as these are robust enough to get you through a quarter before having to push out another one. If you've got a lengthy resource in this format, release it at the beginning of the quarter then use it to fuel the rest of your content strategy for those intervening months.

Pull segments, paragraphs or sections and re-purpose them into shorter blog posts or emails. All you'll need is a new headline, introduction and conclusion plus perhaps a few minor text alterations. Link these shorter content pieces to your full white paper as a call to action.

Videos

Videos are a visual way of storytelling which captivates audiences. Videos are unique in their ability to show more than just text, images or audio. They physically demonstrate your services, solicitors and barristers.

Every day, we're bombarded with a stream of marketing messages. Videos stand out because they condense lots of information into an easy-to-understand format and can be viewed any time, any place, any device by increasingly mobile audiences.

Current YouTube statistics indicate 1 billion unique user visits and 6 billion hours of video are watched each month. Showcasing your videos on this busy platform could prove an extremely lucrative means of lead generation and profile building.

In addition to YouTube, your videos can be uploaded onto other platforms, embedded into your own website, posted onto your blog and utilised in email campaigns to make the most of your investment in their production.

So, if the play button is the most compelling call to action on the web, isn't it time you began recording some videos of your own? Here are some beginner's tips:-

Identify your best performing content from other channels

Analyse the posts on your blog or topics from your email (and other communications) campaigns which have generated the most interaction or click-throughs. Think about your typical buyer persona. Apply strategic, buyer-centric thinking. Your videos should directly address your viewers' requirements and concerns. Also, list the 5-10 questions you get asked repeatedly. With this done, you've got your video subject.

Involve third-party speakers

Ideally, videos should feature clients – past and present – whose opinions are more objective and, therefore, highly valued and trusted by viewers. Even better, renowned industry figures. These are more impartial, and viewers will take definite note of what they're saying.

Run multi-touch, multi-channel campaigns

What are the various ways you can reach out to your clients and prospects – social media, direct mail, email, telemarketing, print adverts etc.? Which combination would work most effectively together? Use direct and indirect, online and offline methods centred around your video resource.

Work out the return on investment

Use a clear methodology such as the lead-to-revenue framework. If possible, compare key metrics for video and non-video campaigns to really realise the benefits of your investment in video marketing.

Decide self or professional production

Remember that you don't necessarily need to involve a professional (potentially expensive) videographer. Instead, you could use the video and audio features in PowerPoint for a visual slide show with voiceover. Go to 'Insert'. 'Video' and 'Audio' are located to the far right of the top toolbar in the 'Media' section.

Conclusion

As you'll have gathered by now, there are overlaps between these communication methods. For example, all require great content. Content probably consumes the lion's share of a marketer's workload so take the concept of "waste not, want not" to another level. You could use the same content matter for every platform, adapted accordingly.

It isn't cheating. In fact, it's an opportunity to put a fresh coat of paint on an old – but highly reliable – machine, and make sure new audiences see earlier content at more convenient times or places. So recycle to your heart's content!

With the introduction of GDPR, you face onerous data protection obligations so don't abuse the personal data held on your clients and prospects. We cover this topic in depth in our 'Preparing for GDPR' chapter.

The main takeaways from this chapter are:-

1. Keep recipients at the forefront of your mind at all times. Stick to what's in it for them by providing solutions to their everyday needs. Put yourself in their shoes when writing content.

2. Schedule your activities. Get organised and take control. This may necessitate allocating responsibilities to particular individuals so that your communication campaigns can go to plan.

3. Select your medium then follow our guidance for each of these unique platforms. The optimum writing style on one is drastically different to that on another. That said, the same theme may run throughout.

4. Pay attention to every seemingly trivial detail. Whether it's allocating sufficient copywriting time for the title of your emailer or using stamps on your mailing envelopes, it's the minutiae that'll catch the eye of your recipients.

5. Consider other variables too. This includes everything from day of the week and time of the day to formatting and design. Try to see the full picture.

6. Track interaction. Some will come to nothing but others will result in new work. Tracking is the tricky part, and there are no hard and fast rules about how best to do it. Whether you use dedicated campaign management solutions, CRM (customer relationship management) software or good-old Microsoft Excel, if there are responses to log, do it.

7. Learn from your mistakes and successes. Any self-respecting marketer wants to improve with experience. Use the insights from your campaigns to fine tune future communications.

CHAPTER FOUR
SOCIAL MEDIA
STRATEGIES

Okay, we've already established that this is no book of theory, but it's good to understand how everything fits together. Social media's another element of the promotion aspect of the marketing mix. Essentially, social media marketing's about communication too. Unlike other methods of communication, though, the conversations take place in an online capacity.

Social media's not to be ignored. Its phenomenon continues to spread throughout the world. To quote a few figures, 2017 user statistics show that Facebook has 2.2 billion monthly active users, Twitter's average is 330 million monthly active users and LinkedIn boasts 546 million members.

On social channels, individuals will talk to others about the quality of your services, particularly if their experience was at the high end of the satisfaction spectrum – in other words, those who felt that the legal advice and representation received was extremely positive.

Conversely, the same is true of disparaging comments and an embarrassing public dressing down can be deeply damaging to your law firm's reputation. This is the downside. You have no control over what people say about you. What you can do, though, is monitor, respond and engage through constructive dialogue.

Some basics before we delve into the nitty gritty of the major social platforms…

First, you should use social media for your press releases, video tutorials, slideshows, industry articles, white papers, quarterly statistics, legal news etc. In other words, you need to provide valuable content that's relevant to your audience's needs.

Second, as users of social media have a tendency to skip around channels, adopt a multi-channel approach to make sure you reach them, wherever they happen to be spending their time at any given moment. Integrated marketing, remember.

This chapter will now cover:-

- Social media guidelines

- Blogging

- LinkedIn

- Facebook

- Twitter

- Google+

- YouTube

- Hootsuite

Social media guidelines

Here are a few simple, but crucial dos and don'ts which should act as your golden rule book for social media marketing:-

<u>Do</u>

- Check and adjust your privacy settings to feel comfortable with what you're sharing on each network

- Be authentic by identifying yourself using your name and company name, where possible, as social media users are wary of anonymous posts

- Mind your manners and show respect to all those engaging with you online by allowing them to speak up too

- Following on from the above, give followers an opportunity to talk so you don't monopolise conversation

- Maintain confidentiality of 'internal only' information however difficult this may sometimes seem

- Invest time and energy to contributing meaningful content which positions you as an expert in the community

- Keep up with 'hot' topics and trends as they may be 'cold' tomorrow!

- Measure your efforts by using analytics and adjust your posts as needed

- Use images and multimedia such as videos so that you 'show' as well as 'tell' and bring your messages to life

- Interact with the good as well as the bad according to your customer service policies and practices

- Thank your brand enthusiasts then retweet, repost, share and like these positive comments

- Have fun because social interactions should be just that!

Don't

- Engage in inflammatory or inappropriate discussions about law firms or barristers' chambers because it's unprofessional and you wouldn't want the same to happen to you

- Use potentially offensive or insensitive content to protect your organisation's brand

- Reference clients, partners or suppliers without their prior approval otherwise they may object

- Post anything unless you want it to linger on the web forever because removing it is nigh-on impossible

- Spam your followers with constant, rambling, self-promotional, one-sided conversation

- Ignore bad feedback as the best response is to initially apologise and attempt to take the interaction offline to resolve properly

- Give up after a short time because social media marketing rarely delivers instant results

The thing that really drives your campaigns is great content. And marketing on social media is free unless you pay for advertising or to boost your posts. The only cost is your time in writing content. So, to make an impact, the key characteristics of good content include:-

- Engaging: Offer something new, whether it's a different perspective, fresh insight or something helpful

- Based on a customer need: Assist your followers with overcoming their challenges

- Integrated: Create a consistent, multi-dimensional brand experience so your message is more likely to hit home

- Search friendly: Think keywords and representative images to get picked up on Google

- Shareable: The easier, the better, as this will extend your reach

- Authoritative: Stand up and be noticed to raise your personal and company profile

- Reflect your brand: Adhering to your guidelines is vital to increase brand awareness

- Contain a clear call to action: Tell your followers what to do next so you don't waste your efforts

- Varied categories: Mix up your posts using evergreen (long term), topical (short term) or calendar specific (date defined) content

Blogging

Bloggers are a community bound together by trust in a fairly sheltered environment. A typical blog incorporates text, images, links to other blogs or websites and may feature media such as podcasts or videos. Usually they're interactive in format so readers can post comments too. One blogger is able to influence many others instantly. Posts are presented in reverse chronological order, with the most recent update first.

There are many reasons to blog including establishing thought leadership to be seen as a knowledgeable expert, humanising your organisation by making your staff clearly visible externally, keeping up to date with changes and developments in the legal world, expanding your audience by engaging with those not present in offline channels, achieving instantaneous one-to-many broadcasting which is difficult with other marketing mediums and improving search engine optim-isation as posts are indexed by Google, Yahoo etc.

It's time to make a place for yourself in the blogosphere in order to:-

- Monitor what people are saying about the legal market, you, your law firm, lawyers and services: Use readily available tools to track and analyse social media interaction such as socialmention.com (http://www.socialmention.com/), Hootsuite (https://hootsuite.com/en-gb), Google Alerts (https://www.google.co.uk/alerts) and blog search engines (try http://www.blogsearchengine.org/).

- Participate in conversations by commenting on other blogs: As a starting point, visit Law Actually (http://lawactually.blog-spot.co.uk/) and Legal Futures (http://www.legalfutures.co.uk/blog).

- Begin to shape conversations by creating and writing your own blog: Use widely used software such as WordPress (http://wordpress.com/) and encourage your staff to actively blog. It's wise to consider some general guidelines, not too prescriptive, in keeping with your corporate image. Keep blog posts short, niche, interesting, authentic and, occasionally, controversial to spark debate. Be transparent and credit sources or blog contributors with their content.

The 5 key elements of your blog are:-

1: A clear objective:
Ask yourself two vital questions: What's this blog's purpose? Who is it for? By putting a detailed blog strategy in place, you'll know who you want to talk to, how often and what you hope to achieve by doing so.

2: Good content:
Following on from the above, plan your content. The best approach is an editorial calendar with pre-agreed blog titles and images so you know what's being posted, on which date, and by whom.

3: Attractive layout:
Web surfers expect blogs to look different from your usual web pages. For this reason, you may wish to use a separate content management system. WordPress is by far the most popular blogging platform (see URL above).

4: Visible social share buttons:
You'll want to make sure content is easily shareable so build in social share buttons to each blog post. As well as helping spread the news of your blog, these buttons provide an indication of the most valuable content (entries with the highest number of shares) showing that it's worth reading.

5: Obvious calls to action:
To optimise on your blog-writing efforts, call your audience to action, for example, request their email address in return for further material (fact sheet, white paper etc.).

LinkedIn

Used by both individuals and businesses to market ourselves and our companies, LinkedIn's always in professional mode. Therefore, while it's important to be friendly, act accordingly. Maintain a professional standard and keep the more informal, chatty posts for other social sites.

You can create personal LinkedIn profiles and company pages. We'll tackle each type in turn...

<u>Personal LinkedIn profiles</u>

It's highly likely that plenty of your organisation's barristers, clerks, senior managers, lawyers and support staff already have a LinkedIn presence. If they're strong, coherent profiles, you're on to a winner as you're presenting yourselves as an expert, unified team. If this isn't the case – whether it's that very few of your staff are on LinkedIn or that the profiles which do exist are of varying quality – some gentle encouragement and guidelines distributed around your organisation wouldn't go amiss.

Here's what personal profiles should feature:-

Photograph: Even on a professional level, people like dealing with people. Getting a good photo of yourself isn't difficult with the plethora of smartphones and other devices we use, all of which have high-tech camera technology embedded within them. Wear business clothes, smile, and take a shot of your head and shoulders.

Headline: This appears in LinkedIn search results so use it wisely. It defaults to your current job title. Edit and change to a succinct sentence which describes what you do and how you can help other LinkedIn users.

Summary: Be authentic (false claims stand out a mile) and, as well as describing your sector experience and personality, also outline the benefits you offer clients and prospective clients of your organisation. Sum up your experience and personal qualities in a few short sentences.

Sound friendly, approachable and knowledgeable to encourage new contacts to connect with you.

Other profile areas: Populate the 'Experience', 'Education', 'Volunteer Experience', 'Skills & Endorsements', 'Accomplishments' (covering 'Organizations', 'Certifications' and 'Publications' etc.) sections. But be selective about the information you upload about yourself. If you've had lots of jobs, don't list them all, especially not the more junior roles, and think about bundling some together under one heading. Make it easy for people to scan your profile and instantly understand your career history, qualifications and how to get in touch. A short synopsis is all that's needed with key career highlights and achievements. Add audio-visual collateral throughout.

Connections: The more people you connect with, the greater the benefits for your business. Personalise your connection invitation message to encourage positive response. Link building is a continuous process so that whenever you make a new acquaintance, connect with them on LinkedIn. Utilise the 'People you may know' feature (you'll find this under 'My Network' in the top toolbar) and see which people LinkedIn is recommending you connect with based upon direct, second and third-degree connections.

Similarly, look at your connections and see who's in their network, then invite pertinent contacts to join yours. A quick word of warning though: don't just connect with others for the sake of connecting. It's not advisable to connect with an individual you've never had a conversation with, either online or offline.

Recommendations: It's readily acknowledged that recommendations are the best form of marketing there is, so this area's pretty important too. The way to gather recommendations is to recommend others and hope that they'll reciprocate. You'll find that the majority will do so. It's bad practice (and slightly rude) to request recommendations from all and sundry. Give something first and they're likely to give something back in return.

The same concept applies to 'Skills & Endorsements'. Reciprocal exchanges are common. Endorse connections for their skills and you'll find that most will endorse you in return.

Groups: Find out which groups your peers are part of and ask to join. If you're unsure which groups to target, let LinkedIn recommend them for you. Once your request's submitted, await moderator approval. This is typically a quick procedure, so within a day or so, you could be contributing to discussions, posting status updates and links, and even asking your own questions.

Thereafter, take part in the conversations. Again, don't blast group members with marketing. You'll annoy everyone and risk getting banned from the group for poor etiquette. Instead, offer advice, comment on others' posts and generally show your subject area knowledge.

And, when confident enough, why not devise your own groups? You can lead discussions and demonstrate thought leadership by keeping followers informed about industry news, as well as undertaking surveys, promoting events etc. LinkedIn groups are where the real networking happens.

With concerted effort, you'll soon have an all-star strength profile.

<u>Company pages</u>

Next, create a company page. You need a personal LinkedIn profile to do this. Go to 'Work' in the top toolbar then click 'Create a Company Page' from the drop down list. Your company page should be a mini version of your website so that those interested in discovering more about your firm can from within LinkedIn. Here's what to do:-

Tell the story of your firm: For your 'Company Description', use your website's 'Home' or 'About us' pages as a starting point. Bear in mind your keywords to boost SEO performance. You'll want your followers to be able to read a high-level overview of your firm, its mission and areas of expertise.

Use images: With your overall firm's branding your foremost consideration, select representative images. Your firm's logo will appear next to your name at the top of the page. Dimension requirements are 300 x 300 pixels. Your main image reflects your business. This should be 646 x 220 pixels.

Add specialties: You're allowed up to 20 items in the 'Specialties' section but it doesn't mean you must fill all 20 available spaces with generic terms. Again, for SEO reasons, list a handful of keyword-specific specialties. You'll rank higher on Google and people will find your organisation more easily. The more specific the phrase, the better.

Keep your company page up to date: Don't set up your page then let it lie stagnant. Update by going to 'Me' in the top toolbar then click on your company which should be listed under 'Manage' in the drop down list. Select 'Edit' and 'Edit page', then populate accordingly. Only designated administrators can perform this function. Once you're done, click on the 'Publish' button in the right hand corner.

Create showcase pages: Every one of your LinkedIn followers isn't interested in every one of your legal area specialisms. Taking the place of the old 'Products / Services' tab, showcase pages allow you to develop customised pages for various target audiences and ultimately develop niche communities around them. LinkedIn members can actually follow these without following your overall company page. You can then tailor content to your heart's content. You're permitted 10 showcase pages per parent company page. This is ideal for your legal area specialisms or business units.

To set up a showcase page, click on the arrow next to the 'Admin tools' button located in the top right hand corner of your company page and select 'Create Showcase Page' from the drop-down list presented. Note: you'll need to have established your company page first. Assign administrators, and work your way through the wizard-like screens. Click 'Publish' at the end to make your showcase page live.

Post compelling content: Get into the habit of posting content regularly. It's about providing valuable resources and nuggets of information which your audience craves. This doesn't have to be freshly written content each time. Sharing articles posted by industry spokespeople is equally acceptable and requires much less effort on your part.

Post content through the 'Share an article, photo, video or idea' area on your company page. These posts will then appear on your home screen and your followers' news feeds. Consider optimum time of day (mornings are generally preferred), length of post (keep it snappy with a link for more information) and imagery (posts with images stand a greater chance of being noticed). Use photos or stock images always and videos where possible (more on this later).

Attract followers: Your content will do much of the work for you but you also need to request that your employees list your organisation as their present employer and follow your company page to drum up more quality followers. They can request new followers via LinkedIn's InMail messaging system, their email signature, PowerPoint presentations and during face-to-face conversations.

Maximising your firm's presence on LinkedIn won't happen overnight. Persistence and patience are vital. After all, the best things in life come to those who wait!

Finally, if you have some spare marketing budget, on a paid-for basis you can upgrade to a premium subscription for additional functionality such as leveraging the wider LinkedIn network to really grow your connections and find top talent. Advertising on LinkedIn is another option, and adverts can be closely targeted based upon user demographics including industry sector, job title, geography and profession. For this purpose, you could take a look at sponsored content, sponsored InMail or display advertising products.

Facebook

Facebook's similar to LinkedIn in that you need an individual profile before a company page. If you think Facebook is for the younger generation only to interact with their friends, organise their social life and post photos of themselves generally having a good time, think again. Facebook users interact with work colleagues and companies, as well as friends, and the number of company pages is growing rapidly. Cast your mind back to those 2.2 billion monthly active users mentioned earlier. In case you still have any lingering doubts, statistically speaking, Facebook is too big to ignore.

Whilst this is something that legal service providers still often shy away from, it's becoming increasingly important in generating awareness and instructions. Facebook users represent a promising audience for your marketing efforts.

By establishing a company page, a corporate community can be developed and public or private (one-to-one) conversations held.

To set up a company page on Facebook, log in to your personal account, click on the down arrow located to the right of your screen and choose 'Create Page'. First choose a classification from the 6 available options. We recommend 'Company, Organization or Institution'. Choose your category from the drop-down list, enter your company name and click the 'Get Started' button.

Follow the Facebook prompts to enter information about your company including a brief description, URL, address and unique Facebook web address. Enhance with imagery by using your logo and other recognisable brand images as your profile picture and cover photo. Click 'Save Info' and your sparkly new page is ready to go.

Thereafter, assign administrators, edit your page content, monitor activity and respond to personal messages via your administration panel. This way, you can continually improve your Facebook presence.

Next it's down to the important stuff. You're ready to create your first post. Posts can comprise updates, questions, industry commentary, photos and videos, and they'll appear in your followers' news feeds. The news feed is what Facebook is all about, as this is where your followers spend their time sharing their own posts and reading those of others.

It's vital to keep your posts short and snappy, and use visual resources. You add posts in the 'Status' section in the middle of the page. You'll see a box with 'Write something…' inside it. Overwrite with your own wording and include a URL for additional information. Use the icons situated underneath the text box to upload a supporting image (recommended!), assign an action or feeling to your status update, and use your location. The latter would be useful if you're posting from an industry event. Finally, 'Publish' to make your news live. It's also possible here to schedule posts for the future or backdate to an earlier point in time. Use the down arrow for this functionality.

Once you're regularly posting, invite people to like your Facebook company page. You can do this by the usual channels or via Facebook itself. Click on the '…' button in the middle of your page and select 'Invite Friends' from the drop down list. Outside of Facebook, utilise your email signature, website, marketing collateral and business cards to drive traffic to Facebook and encourage people to 'Like' your page.

Setting up a company page is free of charge, however, with a bit of cash, you can invest in promotions to further grow your follower base and advertise your services to Facebook users, targeted by location, gender, age and interests. Go to 'Promote' on the left of your screen, select the service required and work through the wizard tabs to create your promotion. This will include setting a budget for your spends.

All adverts go through an approval process from Facebook. You'll get a notification when your advert's ready. When it's running, you can monitor performance via the activity tab of your page. Go to 'Settings' and 'Activity Log'.

The 'Custom Audience' feature bears some similarities, letting you target adverts to carefully defined audience groups comprising people you already know.

Facebook provides user prompts throughout the custom audience set-up process. Once established, these contacts will stay together as a group. The theory is, you're able to target specific customers or prospects at scale and with accuracy, so your advert can reach highly engaged people en masse.

Twitter

Twitter's the networking platform whereby users post tweets comprising a maximum of 280 characters, recently increasing the limit from 140 characters. It's a microblog which hosts short pieces of digital content containing text, images, videos and hyperlinks.

Twitter's a much more spontaneous site on which users post 'what I'm doing right now' type updates so they're often the first place to hear real-time breaking news. For this reason, you need to be there too, otherwise you're missing out.

The benefits of Twitter, then, include:-

- Speed with which news items can be posted as it demands less time and effort

- Messages such as daily news, company updates, industry announcements, re-purposed content (shared from other sites) and other golden nuggets of information can reach thousands of followers in seconds

- Empowers users with mobile access due to its portable nature

- Easily digestible content because posts are short and informally written

- Trending topics help users to stay abreast of current events and get involved in relevant conversations

- Ability to schedule posts for any time, day or night, which is particularly useful during holidays when you want to maintain an online presence

The other major advantage of Twitter relates to increased search engine visibility. Since Twitter and Google announced their partnership early 2015, there's close integration between the two sites. Twitter content, in the form of tweets and hashtags, feed through into Google search results.

Establish your Twitter presence

To get tweeting, set up a company page. This shows the rest of the world who you are. Every element should contain your best content and reflect your identify because first impressions count.

The four components of your Twitter profile are:-

1. Your username: Otherwise known as your Twitter handle. Up to 15 characters in length, this should be something that makes it easy for Twitter users to find you.

2. Your profile photo: as your main profile image and something that'll appear alongside every tweet you post, this is important. Often, company logos are used here as it's a small square space. 400px x 400px to be precise.

3. Your company overview (or bio): You're restricted to 160 characters so get to the point quickly. Concisely describe what your company does and what makes you special. This will entice people to follow you so it's got to work hard. You can also add your location, website URL and other useful information.

4. Your header photo: Recommended dimensions are 1500px x 500px. This is essentially your company's billboard. Make it representative and striking.

Tweet and pin

Post regular tweets relating to your business, areas of law and the wider legal industry. When on the home screen, simply click in the 'What's happening?' box, type your content, upload a photo or video, add a hyperlink and click the 'Tweet' button. Your tweets will be displayed on your profile page and delivered to your followers' timelines.

Writing 280 characters may sound easy, but it can prove difficult to adhere to these length restrictions. Choose every letter painstakingly to get your message across in a coherent and professional way. Insert links to your website or blog where your followers can find more detailed information on the subject. If it helps, use URL shortening tools to save vital space when embedding links into your tweets.

If you go over the character count, Twitter will tell you by showing you a minus number at the bottom of your tweet and won't allow you to post until it's rectified, and either back to zero or a positive number.
You can use the 'Add poll' to include a Q&A, and 'Add location' to show where you are at the time of posting.

You can pin tweets to keep important items at the top of your timeline. To do this, click on the down-facing arrow situated at the top of a posted tweet then choose 'Pin to your profile page' from the drop down list. By doing so, your followers can't fail to miss your important news.

Interact with other Twitter users

Keep on top of others' tweets and use the 'Reply', 'Retweet' and 'Like' facilities to pass along news items which you think your followers should read. You'll find these three icons underneath each tweet in your timeline. Always acknowledge the source of the original tweet rather than trying to pass it off as your own.

Use hashtags

The final point to mention is use of hashtags. These are keywords or phrases which are prefixed with the hashtag symbol (#). Hashtags can be used anywhere in a tweet – beginning, middle or end – but can't contain any spaces or punctuation. They categorise tweets, make searching for topics easier and identify trending topics from popular hashtags.

In essence, that's it, except to say you can view trending topics from the 'Trends for you' area on your home page, and see your page notifications such as new followers and retweets on the appropriately titled 'Notifications' tab, and send direct messages to your followers in the equally well-named 'Messages' tab, both of which are in your top toolbar. And, just like Facebook and LinkedIn, you can use Twitter Ads to advertise your wares to a targeted demographic.

Google+

We don't want to repeat the same content throughout this chapter, so it's enough to say that, like all social networks, Google+ helps businesses to connect with a community of customers and fans. If nothing else, Google+ should not be overlooked because of its significant impact on SEO. Companies using Google+ are more visible in organic search results, typically given top listings by Google. And, as we all know, it's websites on the first page of Google that generate the most clicks.

Now, even non-Google+ account holders can interact with your brand by leaving reviews and sharing their experiences with your firm. This is a great way to improve your credibility and reputation. And, with an estimated 300 million monthly active users, that's a wide reach.

For maximised community engagement, you can organise your connections and share relevant content. This is the way to secure +s, re-shares and replies.

To create a business account, go to the Google My Business web page at https://www.google.co.uk/business. Click on the three-dash icon in the top left hand corner and select 'Join Google+'. You may need to task an administrator of your business email and website accounts (in other words, one of your IT technicians) to enable the service before you can proceed.

In the process of setting up your business page, you'll be prompted to select your business type then work through various form fill requests where you'll add relevant details. Think imagery, accuracy and keywords.

Once you're live, these are the features of Google+ to take note of:-

- Circles: organise people into groups such as customers or influencers then message them

- Collections: follow and share content on specific topics i.e. your area specialties

- Communities: connect with likeminded people with the same interests

- Posts: add content which is keyword-rich and includes images, hashtags, calls to action and links to additional related blog posts or website pages

- Hangouts: hold conversations, host webinars and offer live training to keep in touch with your audience

- Sharing buttons: use the +1 button on your blog and website to encourage sharing

In sum, Google+ may not be as glamorous as Facebook or Twitter but it's a social networking powerhouse, as its user volumes suggest, so get yourself on there.

YouTube

Video marketing has changed from a nice-to-have to an essential part of your marketing mix. Marketers recognise that campaigns incorporating videos are more successful than those without. Visual media appeals to our limited attention spans and time-challenged lifestyles.

If any campaign's going to go viral, it's one with a video. This effectively means they've been shared and reached far more than your intended recipients.

Videos focused on delivering value to viewers are watched, shared and liked most; as opposed to videos waving the corporate flag. For tips on video content, refer to the 'Videos' section in our 'Ensuring Successful Communications' chapter.

YouTube is widely recognised as the world's top video site, attracting 80 million unique users and more than 1.5 billion monthly active users. You can upload videos up to 15 minutes in duration (longer for users with a good track record) in most container formats. Videos can even be uploaded from mobile phones.

Getting started is as easy as any other social network. Here are a few basics to get the ball rolling:-

- Go to https://www.youtube.com/ and click on the 'Sign In' button on the top right hand corner of the screen. As YouTube is now owned by Google, if you already have a Gmail account, you'll automatically have a YouTube account. If not, create an account here from the red 'Create a new Google Account' button.

- Now you've got an account, let's progress to videos. Click on the 'Upload' (up-facing arrow) icon at the top of the screen. Select your video, mark as 'Public' or 'Private' and wait while the video renders.

- When the video upload process is complete, use the site's built-in analytics. Click on the down-facing arrow next to 'Upload'.

You'll see all manner of categories including number of video views and subscriber demographics.

- Finally, have a response plan should your genuine, innocent videos fall foul of commenters and trolls (that's people who post offensive statements, just for the hell of it). If you reply, tread very carefully. The best approach may be to block their account.

Hootsuite

Even your most reliable employees need a holiday and it's impossible to plan for sickness. You can schedule your social media posts in advance. So, if you're due some time off work, your social media marketing doesn't have to stop with you.

There's also the monitoring aspect of seeing the conversations people are having about your business on social media (and, ultimately, take part!). For both jobs, use Hootsuite. It claims to be the most widely used social relationship management platform. It's free for up to 3 social profiles; thereafter it's chargeable but easily affordable.

Go to https://hootsuite.com/en-gb/ to sign up then link your accounts using the 'Add Social Network' button at the top of your screen. There-after, Hootsuite's all about streams. Use the 'Add Stream' button to personalise your screen view. For example, you may wish to see a stream for 'My Tweets' or 'Scheduled' to keep an eye on your own activity. To monitor the activity of others, something such as 'Mentions' or 'Retweets' is useful.

When you're more competent on Hootsuite, you can set up your own reports via the 'Analytics' section of the left hand toolbar. Just as with any marketing exercise, analysing the effectiveness of your campaigns is mandatory. But there's a huge sea of data available to you, so link your social media plans to your overall business objectives and monitor the relevant metrics only. Don't get obsessed with like and follower volumes. These are often considered vanity metrics and of no real value in understanding your social successes.

There's more to Hootsuite. Check out the options in the left toolbar to unleash its full potential.

Conclusion

There's a lot been covered in this chapter but it's not an exhaustive list of social sites. There are more – Instagram, Pinterest, Tumblr, Flickr and Snapchat to name a few – and the list continues to grow as our habits change. Keep abreast of which sites are being used by the types of people you're keen to connect with. If needs be, get on board too.

Hopefully, you should have learned:-

1. Your target audience inhabits more than one social platform. So should you. Use all the tools at your disposal and run fully integrated social campaigns.

2. Utilise the various social channels to tell people what's going on in your business by all means, but also listen and respond. Other social users have a voice too.

3. Don't stress about having to write an unmanageable series of new content. Sharing and commenting takes less time and is no less important.

4. Never say anything online that you wouldn't say in person for self-preservation reasons. Once it's done it can't be undone.

5. Follow our dos and don'ts in order to conduct yourself appropriately. Just because social's more informal, doesn't mean you should throw out the behavioural rule book.

6. It may sound contradictory to #5, but enjoy yourself and have some fun. Where the subject matter permits, lighten the mood. Your engagement levels will soar as a result.

7. Use engagement metrics to track your efforts on social media. Comments per post, likes per post and shares per post give by far the best insights.

8. Marketing and testing go hand in hand. Post, test, refine, test… and repeat ad infinitum.

CHAPTER FIVE
WHAT MAKES A WINNING WEBSITE?

When Tim Berners-Lee invented the World Wide Web in 1990, I'm sure even the computer scientist himself couldn't have envisaged the phenomenon it is today. The total number of websites live on the internet is estimated to be around 1.8 billion. That's a lot of sites vying for the ever-dwindling attentions of modern web surfers.

Just how can you make your website stand out from the other masses of law firms' and chambers' websites? A mediocre website doesn't demand (or deserve) to be noticed above the others. And not getting noticed is bad for business.

From a marketing perspective, it's pointless attempting to drive huge volumes of traffic to your website if, when they arrive, your content's so poor that it causes them to leave (or bounce as it's better known) straightaway. Similarly, it's pointless having the best content on the internet if no one can find your website.

The process of improving visibility is search engine optimisation (SEO). The engagement factor is tackled by on-page content. The highest-performing websites do both of these marketing activities in tandem.

That's what we're covering in this chapter – the intricacies of SEO in its many forms including pay-per-click (PPC) advertising, writing copy which lengthens your visitors' stay, and monitoring traction via analytics.

Read about the following topics here:-

- SEO

- PPC

- Landing pages

- Newsfeeds

- Google Analytics

SEO

Over the years, Google's algorithms (that's the criteria Google uses to decide the relevance of your site according to search terms used) have become cleverer in the way they rank websites. For example, recently introduced Google updates mean websites are rewarded with higher rankings if they're device-responsive (Mobile Friendly Update), contain quality content (Panda Update) and have a series of genuine links (Penguin Update).

But the basics first. A keyword is a word or sequence of words that a search engine uses to index web pages when browsers type them into the search bar to locate companies, products or services.

Typically, boosting your ranking on search engines is done by a combination of organic and paid keywords tactics. With PPC, costs are constant. You need to keep paying to appear against certain keywords and ultimately outbid your competitors.

For organic success, however, it's about writing content that will index well and drive revenue-boosting traffic your way. The way to perfect organic listings is on-page SEO. This is the wording on every page of your website and each page's metadata. The former needs no explaining. The latter is text such as your page titles and page descriptions. On-page titles in your website influence your page rankings too. These are called your title tags.

Here's our usual round-up of tips for SEO:-

- Do your keyword research: Find out what your prospects are searching for. Use a free tool, such as Google Trends, to identify which words people are using for searches on Google. Go to www.google.com/trends, type in terms or keywords and find out their related search frequency, volume and location.

- URLs: Keep your URLs short and keyword rich. The first 3-5 words carry most weight.

- Titles: Where possible, start titles with strong keywords (rather than use them in the middle or end). Optimal length is 50-60 characters so that titles display properly and in their entirety. Choose words tactically as these titles are the first impression many people have of your page and its relevance to their needs. Use one H1 (main) title tag with H2 and H3 (sub) title tags throughout.

- Multimedia: Images, videos and diagrams reduce bounce rate and increase time on site thereby influencing Google ranking factors.

- Outbound and inbound links: Links between external related authority sites boost a page's rank. Build your links legitimately. Not all links are equal. One link from an established, authoritative website is better than 100 from slightly questionable, newly launched sites. Create shareable content, submit press releases, post on blogs and establish business partnerships. These activities will result in links to your site. Linking social media posts on your company pages to related content on your website plays a huge part as well.

- Interlinking: Employ an intelligent interlinking strategy to link content from one page to other pages on your website. Use targeted anchor text. This is the actual text used for the link.

- Keyword-rich first 100 words: Use your keywords from the outset to emphasise your page is all about those subjects.

- Loading speed: This is another ranking signal so ensure pages are quick to load. Visit Google's PageSpeed Insights at https://developers.google.com/speed/pagespeed/insights, type your URL in the bar and click 'Analyze' to calculate how quickly your pages load. Look at your 'Optimization' and 'Speed' rankings (out of 100) as well as your 'Should Fix' and 'Consider Fixing' lists to resolve any issues.

- Long content: As a general guide, aim for 1500 words per web page, especially when you're targeting competitive keywords.

- Social sharing buttons: Search engines like these buttons plus you'll engage browsers better if they're prominently displayed.

- Bounce rate: Manage your bounce rate by enticing browsers to stay on your site with good copy, straightforward navigation and a clean website design.

- Mobile friendliness: Ensure your layout will automatically respond and adapt to the visitor's screen size so they don't need to zoom in and out. Browsing should be as easy on mobile devices – such as smartphones and tablets – as it is on PCs and laptops. Non-mobile-friendly websites have too-small text and too-close links which lessens the user experience. Test whether your site is mobile friendly using Google's webmaster tools at https://www.google.co.uk/webmasters/tools/mobile-friendly. Results will show the points you need to address. Then use analytics to make decisions about what your mobile version should look like – minimal text, smaller images, fewer menu options and lots of white space.

- HTTPS: In a bid to protect web surfers from cyber attack, Google is prioritising HTTPS (Hypertext Transfer Protocol Secure) URLs over regular HTTP ones. It may be time to redirect your site to a HTTPS version. Obtain a security certificate issued by a certified authority and get your technicians on task to make the shift. When you migrate to HTTPS, Google treats this as a URL change which can temporarily affect your traffic numbers. So be patient.

PPC

As should be clear by now, SEO is the process whereby web copywriters produce content with search engine results in mind. The best copy is that which generates first page listings, preferably in the top five but definitely on page one, and keeps readers on your website once they've clicked through.

Achieving this objective is quite a challenge and is a lengthy process. One way to improve your search engine rankings with immediate effect is through PPC advertising. This is a sure-fire way to enhance your search results by paying to move up rankings.

PPC advertising, otherwise known as sponsored links, appear in prominent areas of search engine pages above organic (natural, non-paid) results. To get listed in these prime positions, you bid against your competitors for keywords that are relevant to your services. However, you only pay when somebody clicks on your advert, hence the name pay-per-click, although other pricing strategies can be adopted (more on this later). If you bid more for relevant keywords than your competitors, your advert will be placed above theirs.

To set up your PPC campaigns, follow these guidelines:-

Define your objectives

What do you want to achieve? Are you just trying to drive traffic to your website or attempting something specific such as getting people to subscribe to your newsletter, download your e-book etc.? Be clear about why you're advertising as this will help you to tailor your advert wording and select the right keywords.

Choose your search terms

The keywords or phrases you bid on must reflect what surfers will type into search engines when looking for legal services like those offered by your business. Be specific and choose long-tail phrases.

Long-tail phrases comprise three or four keywords and represent exactly what you do. The thinking is, if someone uses this highly targeted search request and finds you, they're much more likely to buy your services because you're an exact match. Long-tail keywords are lesser used than shorter, generic keywords but they carry higher conversion rates. 'Barrister Watford immigration' is preferable to 'barristers' chambers'.

Set your budget

Decide what you're willing to pay for your keywords and phrases, remembering that costs will vary with the competitiveness of your market. You can focus your bid strategy on clicks, conversions or impressions. The most common is automated cost-per-click dictated by a maximum daily budget.

Write your advert

Your advert will contain a heading, small amount of text and URL. There are other sections you can utilise too. These are called 'Ad extensions' in AdWords. For example, your sitelink extensions are for highlighting other relevant pages on your site such as your contact form, and will be hyperlinked to the pages in question. There are also callout extensions which allow you to shout about accreditations, awards and the like. There are all manner of extensions available to you. Use what you can to extend your advert beyond your character length restrictions.

Concentrate on giving browsers the information that will encourage them to click through to your website. Also, adhere to the defined length limits, namely 30 characters for heading 1, 30 characters for heading 2, 80 characters for the description and 15 characters for the path (that's your URL). Or, try out Google's new expanded text adverts, rolled out in January 2017, for more characters per field.

Create your landing page

Direct surfers to a landing page that's relevant to your advert rather than just taking them to your home page. These are bespoke web pages containing titles and wording which mirror your advert. Dedicated pages such as these increase the likelihood of conversion (generating a sale) and decrease the number of bounces (people immediately leaving your website).

Make it easy for someone to take the next step, whether that's a subscription, sales enquiry or other call to action. At all times, make it clear how visitors can contact you straightaway.

See the next section for more information on landing pages.

Track your users' journey

Experiment with different keywords, approaches and budgets to discover which generates the best results. Track where users arrive and, once there, how they interact with your site through Google Analytics. It's a free-to-use analysis tool whose sophisticated reports allow you to monitor not only your online advertising, but your entire website. Impressions (how often your adverts appear), click through rate (how often your adverts are clicked on), response rates (how often people respond to your site's offers) are all measured for your different keywords and advert(s).

These insights can be fed back into your AdWords campaigns. Remember the mantra 'test and refine'. The work of a good online AdWords campaign is never done. Using your monitoring data, your keywords, adverts and landing pages can be constantly improved upon. Keep what's working. Amend or lose what isn't working and move on to the next campaign.

Again, see the later section for a walkthrough of Google Analytics.

Landing pages

When visitors arrive on your website, whether it's from organic or paid search results, social media, online directories, referral sites or specific marketing campaigns, even printed adverts, the page they land on is (appropriately) called a landing page. After luring them to your website, don't waste the opportunity to impress. Make your landing pages concise, relevant, compelling and attractive with an obvious call to action or links to the rest of your site.

Before you begin, it's worth noting that there are different types of readers. Complete readers demonstrate unrivalled loyalty by reading pages word-for-word, top-to-bottom. Scanners will make up most of your audience. They read headlines and introductions, stretching to various sub-headings, highlighted terms and images as they skim through. And there's bottom feeders, the most impatient group of the lot, who'll skim read your headline and possibly a couple of sentences, before jumping to the bottom of your page to read your summary.

Your role, as a web copywriter, is to cater for all their needs with word-perfect content, scan-friendly layout and strong supporting imagery so that they'll stick around and, better still, contact you to instruct your solicitors or barristers for work.

Here's how:-

Headline

Your headline needs to be specific and interesting enough to keep visitors reading. Formatting is also critical. A few correctly-placed capital letters and easy-to-read font portray professionalism.

Sub-headings and other formatting

Use various formatting techniques that break up the text and draw the reader's eye to important points, for example sub-headings, bulleted lists and images (or other media) with captions.

The body

Use the main body content to showcase your expertise. Utilise quotes, anecdotes or positive feedback to tell a story and help draw your readers in.

Keep your first paragraph short and sweet. Presenting a huge block of solid text at the outset will just send them running elsewhere. Make sure content is relevant at the time it's posted. Otherwise, your visitors will wander off to more up-to-date sites.

Remember the important details – who, what, when, where, why and how – as these are crucial to good copywriting. And use short words. Simple words communicate better than big words and pompous language or corporate speak. It makes it feel more like a conversation.

Write sentences with positive words i.e. 'Don't get left behind' might become 'Get ahead of the competition'. Sometimes negative language is necessary and adds variety to your copy, but don't overdo it.

Logic influences decision making. Use statistics, research data, case studies, testimonials and other sources to prove what you say is true.

Not a copywriting tip as such but incorporating various media (photos, videos, infographics, slides and more) in your website makes a huge difference.

Conclusion

Your conclusion works in partnership with your headline and should sum up the key message of your page. What happens when your reader's finished your page? Call them to action by requesting they visit another related web page, complete your contact form, download your white paper etc.

Postscript

This is another vital, but often neglected, aspect of your landing page since it's where conversions happen. It should reiterate your message and provide incentives for visitors to take immediate action.

Newsfeeds

Google likes regularly updated websites. By constantly adding new content to your site, you'll be rewarded for your hard work by getting higher search listings. The most popular way of doing this is via a blog (refer to our 'Social Media Strategies' chapter for blogging advice).

But supplying a continuous stream of fresh content for new and repeat visitors to your site is a major challenge and, with an already hectic schedule of work, you may simply not have time to manage a blog as well as everything else on your never-ending to-do list. There's an easy way to maintain a busy blog without writing a single word of content – newsfeeds.

Newsfeeds, otherwise known as RSS (Really Simple Syndication) are a syndicated news service which draws stories on your chosen topics from other websites onto yours. RSS is effectively a coding solution. You get the benefit (and the credit!) of presenting the very latest desired inform-ation with absolutely no effort on your part. Except for the initial set up, hence this tip. Here's how it's done:-

1. Find the source of your news. You'll see RSS feeds all over the internet. Just look for the small orange icon featuring a dot and two waves.

2. Source an RSS feed API (application program interface). Some are free, others are chargeable. Research carefully.

3. Use a standard piece of Javascript code to define the format of your news. This will usually comprise a hyperlinked headline and brief summary for the first news item; and either the same format or just a hyperlinked headline for subsequent news items. This is

effectively the link between the original source of news and your web page.

4. With your code ready, copy onto your desired page, be it your home or interior page, into the head section.

5. See how the news displays on your live web page and customise the code accordingly, for example adjust widths, margins etc. Also, you can update to accommodate new sources of news.

We pride ourselves on practicing what we preach. Take a look at our own newsfeeds in action under 'Other legal sector news' at http://barmarketing.co.uk/news-and-tips.

Google Analytics

Just like any marketing collateral, a website should evolve, not once written and thereafter never reviewed. Updating and adding content is the only way to keep visitors on your site and tempt them to make return visits with the promise of something new to enjoy.

But, this process isn't based on wild guesstimates about what you think would improve your website, engage your browsers and improve inter-action. It should be based on data. Google Analytics is chock-full of data for this very purpose.

Google Analytics shows marketers, in statistical format, how their website's performing. It gathers analytical information from your site so you can monitor visitor interaction such as:-

• How many people have visited your site and where they live

• How they landed on your site (from social networks, search engines, blogs etc.)

• Inbound traffic figures from paid-for Google AdWords campaigns

- Which keywords are being used to find your site

- How much time they spent on your site

- Volumes of new or returning visitors

- Which web browsers and networks they used to access your site

- What technology is adopted by users (desktop, tablet, smartphone)

- Which are your most popular web pages

- Where people are exiting your site

How to set it up

Go to Google Analytics and create an account by filling in basic information about your website.

Next, get your tracking code. Click on the 'Admin' button at the bottom of the left hand toolbar then select 'Tracking Info' and 'Tracking Code'. Copy the tracking ID code, access your content management system and paste it into your site's source code.

Typically, the tracking code is pasted inside the header file. As this is common for all pages, it'll be added automatically to every page on your site.

Google Analytics dashboard

Now that you're set up, you need to familiarise yourself with its features. To begin, access the reporting features within Google Analytics.

The time period can be adjusted by using the drop-down selections in the top right hand corner of the various reporting pages. This defined date range will then apply to all generated reports but can be adjusted again at any time.

Menu choices

The left hand column is the place you'll find links to sections for precise information about your site's visitors, content and performance.

The menu comprises the following:-

- Real-Time: Your web data is being updated constantly in Google Analytics, with just a couple of seconds' delay. This area allows you to monitor visitor activity as it happens so that you can analyse the people on your site right now.

- Audience: The main area is audience which includes graphs, percentages and pie charts on visitors' demographics, interests, geography (language and location), technology, mobile devices and how they flowed through your site to really get to know your audience's characteristics, behaviour and interests.

- Acquisition: Use this section to compare traffic from search (paid or organic), referrals, email and your marketing campaigns to evaluate both the mix and quality of traffic sources.

- Behaviour: Focused on your site's content, performance, search-ability and interactivity, this area helps you to explore how people find and interact with your content.

- Conversions: This area is not automatically activated in Google Analytics. It requires your input to get up and running. It's about setting goals such as minimum session duration, downloaded white papers, registered webinars or completed contact forms, to measure how well your site fulfils its objectives. This is particularly prevalent to e-commerce sites but not to be entirely dismissed for B2B websites.

By working your way through these areas and the sub-sections contained therein, you can understand specifics ranging from the most popular devices and browsers to top landing and exit pages.

All of Google Analytics' statistics provide valuable insights about your site and the visitors it receives. Use the data to introduce improvements to your wording, layout and imagery. For example, if you discover that the bulk of your referrals come via Twitter on Wednesday from posts relating to TUPE, generate more site content on this subject and promote by tweeting mid-week.

Another example could be that the majority of your visitors use smartphones to browse your site. You would need to cater for their needs by producing a mobile-friendly version optimised for these devices or, even better, create an app compatible with iOS, Android and / or Windows phones.

Take another, more obvious example. If your home page is also your highest exit page, there's something drastically wrong with your site. You need to invest resources into spelling out your services, presenting important news and offering clear points of navigation to other key areas. You don't want to lose visitors directly upon entry to your site, otherwise the effort and cost of getting them to your site in the first place has been wasted.

<u>Custom reporting</u>

Once you've mastered the basics, begin to feel confident with Google Analytics and have ambitions to drill down even further into the performance of your site, try custom reports because sometimes the information you want to see isn't available in standard datasets. Be adventurous and give it a try by going to 'Customisation' in the left hand toolbar and working your way through the tabs presented. You can personalise your dashboard, build shortcuts and set up alerts from here too.

Conclusion

Your internet marketing strategy is part of your overall digital marketing plan, and is all about maximising your online presence. At its most basic, your website helps clients find you by showcasing your work and providing contact details. The marketing opportunities that the internet presents, however, go far wider than this.

The key takeaways from this chapter are:-

1. Your website's no use if nobody visits it; utilise a combination of SEO and PPC to maximise visibility.

2. Equally, your website's no use if it doesn't keep those that do visit it engaged; captivating landing pages and constantly updated content via newsfeeds are the way to go.

3. Tracking and reporting on your traffic shows how visitors find and use your website; adopt a 'test-and-refine' attitude, fuelled by insights from Google Analytics, to keep your online collateral in tip-top shape.

CHAPTER SIX
PRESS, PR AND
EVENTS PLANNING

There are multiple methods of promoting your business externally, some paid for and some free. Of course, when we say "free", there is actually an associated cost – your salary. It takes time to plan, write and run any marketing campaign but there aren't any additional costs on top of this. It's extremely rewarding when your projects achieve success, even more so when it's come about as a result of free activity.

In this chapter, we're covering this range of topics, introducing best practice guidelines and often suggesting that a bespoke approach is more effective:-

- Advertising

- Press releases

- Advertorials

- Events

- Webinars

- Directories

- Cause-related marketing

Advertising

The most obvious technique for promoting your business is advertising. This is where you pay for space on a website, billboard, radio, TV, magazine etc. (we'll come back to this later) and create an attractive piece of artwork or narrative to showcase what you do.

According to even the most conservative estimates, we're exposed to between 5,000 and 10,000 marketing messages every day. So many, in fact, that we become largely immune to them. Unless they really stand out.

With a good advert, hundreds, thousands even, of people will have seen / heard, understood and potentially acted upon it. With a bad advert, you've wasted £thousands as well as negatively impacting your reputation (in extreme cases, obviously).

Before we proffer our tips, we're taking you back to marketing basics. You may have heard of the acronym AIDA. Standing for attention, interest, desire, action, it's a methodology applied by copywriters and graphic designers for projects. To elucidate:-

Attention: You've got seconds to attract your reader's, viewer's or listener's attention. Bold headlines, strong images, corporate colours and company logo are essential.

Interest: Present your proposition to turn attention into interest. You could consider presenting some fascinating facts and figures about your organisation, incorporating quotes from happy clients etc.

Desire: Really try to persuade your audience that they need your services by relating a series of benefits and / or accompanying with a special offer. Don't overload with heavy text. Restrict your word count and use bullets for easier reading.

Action: Tell your audience what they should do next in order to step into your sales funnel. From thenceforth, you can engage with them on a more personal level in an attempt to achieving your ultimate goal – converting them to client status.

With the AIDA process in mind, let's take things a stage further with some research, copywriting and design tips to turn your adverts from washout to knockout:-

Do your research

Scan hard copy publications, browse websites, watch the commercial breaks when your favourite programme's on TV and generally open your eyes to the adverts you're seeing every day then request features schedules and rate cards, ask for information regarding readership statistics and profiles, find out about distribution areas and methods, and spot opportunities for additional editorial coverage.

Armed with detailed background research, you're able to choose the best platforms at a cost to suit your budget.

Choose your medium carefully

You can actually target a particular specialised segment with most mediums. There's no point in paying mega bucks for a huge poster on the London underground if your target audience rarely travels by tube. Analyse the demographics within the various media packs.

There really is an abundance of advertising platform options. There's traditional advertising – print, television, radio – and then there's everything else. The "everything else" category includes increasingly popular online banner adverts, Google AdWords campaigns and social media adverts.

Plus there's ambient advertising which is all about placing adverts in unusual places and on unusual items. It could be an advert on a bottle of milk being sold in your supermarket or street art in your local shopping district. Of course, many of these wacky ideas are just not appropriate for professional companies but it's worth keeping your mind open.

Make your message relevant, meaningful and powerful

I saw a sponsor's advert recently at a nearby sports ground. Its main message was "free parking" but the company name was only featured in the URL in small print at the bottom. Free parking is most definitely a bonus but if I don't know who you are or what you do, your parking spaces will remain empty.

Take time to plan your message. What is your objective? To position yourself as a market-leading law firm or barristers' chambers? To inform audiences about your full range of services? To drive traffic to your website? To reinforce the messaging of an integrated campaign?

Once you've identified your aims, let the copywriting process begin.

Plan your copy

Keep text brief, to the point and conversational in style. Think benefits, benefits, benefits. Why should people attend your event, subscribe to your newsletters, trial your services or other message-dependent action? How will they benefit from doing so?

We find that happy client testimonials add credibility. But only use genuine testimonials. And spell check. Spelling mistakes depict poor quality and reflect badly on you.

Create strong visuals

Plan a creative brainstorming session as a starting point then play around with different colours, font types, photos, stock images, illustrations and layout to give your advert optimum visual impact. But don't go overboard with your graphics as your message can get lost in the ensuing chaos.

If the purpose of your advertising campaign is to improve the volume of traffic to your website, you may want to include a quick response (QR) code in your artwork. These are essentially 2D barcodes comprising an arrangement of black modules in a square grid on a white background.

A free imaging app downloaded on a smartphone or tablet enables the user to quickly scan the QR code and be directed straight through to your chosen web page.

<u>Plan your responses and monitor performance</u>

Whatever your call to action, make sure your staff – right down to your receptionist – are briefed in how to handle inbound enquiries and have the capacity to cope, should you find yourself overflowing with responses.

Measure responses to calculate effectiveness and inform future advertising. This could be anything from asking callers where they heard about your organisation to tracking web traffic volumes via Google Analytics. A lot of the time with advertising, it's impossible to measure an actual return on your investment. That's why adverts are mainly used for brand awareness. Be mindful of this.

Press releases

After advertising, the next most-used promotional activity is public relations. This is communicating with your public in order to maintain a favourable image or reputation. Your public encompasses everyone external to your business.

The main bodies are your target audience (that's your prospective clients), the media and other opinion leaders. For the first of these, your communication campaigns are the route to success (see our 'Ensuring Successful Communications' chapter). For the second and third of these, you may be tasked with writing speeches, arranging interviews for your company spokespeople, holding press conferences and so on. Primarily, you'll be writing and submitting press releases.

Press releases are used as a channel into various media, whether it's a niche trade publication or national press, to highlight information in the life of your organisation.

As press releases can often end up in the bin, for the sole reason that editorial teams get overrun with them, here's our usual round-up of advice:-

Know which publications to target

In much the same way as researching for advertising opportunities, find potential publications. Most print publications have supporting websites so the majority of your research can be performed online.

Compile a spreadsheet of publications, editors' contact details, submission deadlines and forthcoming features schedules. Over time, your aim is to develop relationships with editors. Send them a press release relating exactly to that edition's special feature and you'll get a favourable response. Taking the time to plan to the nth degree like this will pay off in terms of column space gained.

Avoid self-praise

While it's tempting to launch into a full narrative of how good you are, think like an editor and reader, and stick to the facts of the matter without overuse of superlatives. Just like direct mail which is often labelled "junk", press releases suffer from the media image of "spin", inferring that your message doesn't represent the absolute truth. It's your responsibility to present the facts without distortion or exaggeration so that the credibility of your press releases is raised.

Consider the tone of your submission – it'll need to be more objective and less salesy. It's not a sales pitch dressed up as a press release.

Tap into the novelty factor

This could be a significant claim such as being the first, latest or biggest, for example winning a landmark case. Similarly, your news will be appealing to the media if it's about conflict, covers a niche or local topic, or is seasonal. Try to be different.

Keep your body content succinct

Fit everything onto one A4 page (of a Word document) if possible, with all the key facts in the first paragraph and the headline summarising the story, to persuade the reader to continue. Follow word counts closely. And, when you're done, check for accuracy – it must be spelling and grammatical-error free. A decision to keep or delete your release will be made within seconds.

Incorporate quotes

Quotes from actual people, ideally a third party, make your story real. Avoid boring and fictional quotes. It has to be original and true.

Use the "Notes to Editors" section

Don't clutter your release with too much detail as this slows down the reader. Place relevant background, technical or legal information at the foot of your release along with contact details.

Keep the momentum going

Positive press coverage helps build your reputation. They act as mailshots, reminding the media of your existence, so send regularly. However, don't just send irrelevant releases to keep to a fixed quota. Make sure you have an important business message to deliver each time.

Add a photograph

One good photograph can seriously improve your chances of publication. Conversely, a poor quality dull photograph will increase your chances of rejection. Brief your photographer.

Get the timing right

Timing is everything. For example, send on Sundays for Monday reading or during public holidays when they have less news items awaiting their attention.

If there are editorial deadlines, give your editor sufficient time to receive, read and allocate space for your press release. If it's sent after deadline, all the allotted spaces will be filled. Being on time speaks volumes about your reliability as a contributor too, which helps cement your standing amongst editors.

Grow relationships with the media

By developing a relationship with specialist or general press, you've got greater access to the potential media spotlight when you need it. Try to speak and meet with contacts. You may want to invite them out to lunch to discuss how you can help each other out. Always acknowledge placement of your articles with a "thank you for the coverage" message.

Plan for crisis management

On very rare occasions, firms are affected by crisis situations i.e. management fallouts or high-profile cases lost. Be alert to possible situations and develop contingency plans so that you can respond appropriately to negative publicity. Be specific about the details to put your readers' minds at ease. Honesty is the best policy to regain the trust of your public.

Keep a log of coverage generated by your submissions. It's useful to know, can be drawn upon in your marketing campaigns and to prove your worth to senior management.

Even if you have the most factual, perfectly written press release, you have absolutely no control over what appears and where (if at all). If you're lucky enough to secure press coverage, the amount of space devoted to your story, and slant adopted, is purely an editorial decision. However, one good paragraph is worth a whole page of advertising, so be proud of any coverage gained.

Advertorials

If your press releases aren't hitting the mark, there's always advertising's upmarket relative but press releases' poor relation, the advertorial. Advertorials typically comprise a story with advert underneath. They're paid for in the same way as adverts, but are much more effective and memorable than a standalone advert. They appear in the style of a regular, objective journalistic or editorial article, but they're not.

The benefit of buying space for advertorials is that you're in complete control of the message. The words you write will appear in their entirety on the printed (or, indeed, online) page. You can usually influence the layout of the advertorial, including use of images and logos. Publications will be happy to send you a PDF proof of the page for review and approval before it's published.

The rules of press release writing apply to advertorials too. Crisp, compact, clear, relevant, timely content is vital.

The additional factors to consider are securing the best deal for your advertising spend and tailoring the accompanying advert to the editorial wording.

Events

Exhibitions, conferences and other events are a great source of fresh new leads. It's true permission-based marketing, bringing potential buyers directly to your stand or in front of your company speaker.

But events don't come cheap. You invest hundreds, if not thousands, of pounds to secure your stand space or run your bespoke event, so here are some tips on making the most of your presence:-

Send "save the date" cards

Which of your staff and speakers are key to the event? Check and synchronise their diaries for a mutually agreeable date and time, then send a "save the date" card or email notification advising them to keep it free for your soon-to-be-held event.

Book a venue

This could be a straightforward task of booking a room in your office or more-involved process of liaising with hotels or other conference room venues for availability and quotes. Make sure you review your options properly by considering everything, from convenience of location to what's provided as part of your room hire arrangement.

Ask yourself: can the venue be easily accessed and is it situated close to network links? Are there enough parking spaces? Put yourself in your attendees' shoes. Where is their likely starting point and where will they continue on to afterwards? Plan their route in your head and choose a location convenient for the majority.

If it's an exhibition you're attending, you'll be in frequent contact with your event organiser.

Enquire about availability

Once you've generated a shortlist of prospective venues, check their availability for your event date(s). To be on the safe side, make a provisional booking to avoid disappointment. There's nothing worse than finding your dream venue only to discover that it's fully booked! However, check about cancellation fees and flexibility in case the date changes. You'll also need to know if extras, such as equipment and accommodation, are available on the date(s) required.

Set your agenda, send your invites and promote your event

You can now plan the format for the event which may involve an introductory welcome, key note session(s), guest speaker(s), refreshment break(s) and more. Set the theme and title, then invite people to attend.

Your invitations could be a glossy postal mailer, website article, social media post or other method. Also, email to your desired attendees.

Then, as a second invitation, don't just re-email your original recipients en masse in the hope of catching the attention of those not yet registered and trying not to annoy (too much) those who have. Exclude those who've booked and those who've rejected the invitation before you touch base again.

As your first email hasn't quite done its job, this invitation should be even more enticing. You could preview content from presentations, add biographies of speakers and highlight some of the more advantageous details such as networking opportunities and after-parties. Lengthier emails are the norm here.

For tips on invitation design, go to our chapter titled 'The Importance of Design'.

<u>Confirm all bookings received and send reminders</u>

Acknowledge recipients' requests to register, reassure them of having made the right decision (to book a place at your amazing event!) and provide a handy reference of the basics relating to the event. Typically you'll attach a map including directions, nearest transport links and car parking facilities. An itinerary and specific instructions (i.e. dress code) are standard fare too.

As your event draws closer, it's advisable to remind delegates of their forthcoming commitment because we're all busy and have a tendency to forget things. This will boost your attendee rates. Ask them to submit any dietary requirements and send questions to speakers in advance. By establishing ongoing pre-event dialogue, conversation will flow more freely when you eventually meet in person.

<u>Brief your internal contacts</u>

So, you've invited your clients and prospects, but remember that your internal contacts need event specifics too. Produce an event brief and circulate accordingly, reminding them of their earlier "save the date" communication. The brief should also be submitted to any guest speakers.

Check out your facilities and catering options

You'll need a clearly defined event agenda to fully define your requirements in the first place. Are you looking for a large main room, with several smaller break-out rooms and separate areas for networking? Can you book a projector, whiteboard, internet access or other audio visual services? Is the seating capacity sufficient and room layout satisfactory?

Can the venue provide refreshments and / or catering? Alternatively, do you need to source outside companies for technical equipment, furniture hire, food and drink supplies?

Devise your layout

At least 60% of your stand should be open, making it easily accessible. Have a clear focal point such as a screen with rolling presentations, coffee bar or pods to sit and chat. Think about your visitors' experience and make it obvious how they should enter, interact, pick up literature, find out what they need and leave the area.

Choose your exhibition equipment

Work out what type of equipment would best accommodate your stand space. It could be a nomadic frame with interchangeable graphics, easy-to-assemble selection of roller banners or fully built shell scheme. No doubt a literature stand and some form of seating would be beneficial as well.

Select jaw-dropping graphics

The first consideration is branding. The look and feel of your stand graphics should mirror the rest of your branded collateral. Second, keep the copy simple. If possible, tailor the wording to the specific sector or event. Third, use powerful imagery for visual impact. Your aim is for visitors to take note, and fully understand who you are and what you do within a few seconds' glance.

Use lighting

Use lights such as spotlights or mood lights and height so that your stand is bright with no dark corners. It'll seem more open and welcoming that way.

Print your stand materials

Do your existing marketing materials satisfy the requirements of your event? Do you need any new documents produced? Are any print levels of your brochures, newsletters, case studies etc. running low? Do you need to replenish your print stocks?

Create your PowerPoint presentation(s)

Even veteran speakers get nervous before presenting. A well-planned, structured presentation will go a long way to helping you feel prepared and banishing those pre-event butterflies. Using PowerPoint presentations as a prop keeps your audience engaged and you on track. There are three factors to consider – design, content and delivery.

As always, design is paramount. The template should be branded so that your organisation is easily recognisable. As a visual medium, images are important. This could range from photos to embedded videos. Your images need to correlate to the words on screen, thus reinforcing your message. PowerPoint performs all sorts of weird and wonderful tricks, however it's not a good idea to pack your presentation full of varied transitions and animations. Use these special effects sparingly.

Next, content. We propose that every good presentation has 4 elements: introduction, key points, examples and recapping. Keep content short and punchy. Use the "notes" section of the PowerPoint for detailed content as a speaking prompt. This is the area which your audience won't see. If you cram loads of text-heavy slides into your PowerPoint and simply read the words on screen, your audience will switch off. Whatever you do, check the accuracy of your content. Don't present incorrect information or statistics.

Finally, delivery. Don't just become a slave to your PowerPoint. The best presentations are conversations, not monologues, so build in lots of opportunities for audience participation. Ask questions and invite questions from the audience. Speak loudly and clearly, just as you would in court. Maintain eye contact with audience members.

To repeat the well-known phrase – practice makes perfect. Have a trial run and refine accordingly. This will also help you to avoid overrunning which makes your planning skills appear poor.

<u>Have a hook</u>

Give your staff a reason to approach delegates (i.e. branded water to give away) and delegates an incentive to approach your staff (i.e. competition or prize draw). The more conversation takes place, the more leads you'll generate.

<u>Capture leads</u>

Devise a lead form to be completed during discussions in a concise, legible format, and rank by priority for follow up post event. You'll want to get basic contact details, areas of interest and further information such as stage in buying cycle.

<u>Set a dress and behaviour code</u>

To look more like a unified team, rather than collection of individuals, issue a dress code to your staff. This doesn't necessarily mean a 2-piece suit with matching ties. If the event is casual in nature, the code could be something like black clothes.

Event success is reliant upon the performance of your stand staff. They shouldn't sit reading a newspaper, working on their laptop, chatting huddled together, talking on a mobile phone, eating or drinking. Your staff should be energetic and enthusiastic, as your next big client could come along at any time. Choose staff carefully and keep them motivated. Schedule regular breaks and introduce a bit of gentle competition (i.e. person who logs the most leads wins a bottle of champagne).

Tick off everything on your to-do list

Your preparation may span other, equally important, items. Branded giveaways, stationery, prizes (if you're holding a draw), accommodation, insurance and contingency plans to name a few.

Keep a log of your costs

There's no avoiding the importance of costs. You don't want any nasty surprises when the final invoice arrives in your inbox or through the post. Make sure you're aware, and have agreed to, all the associated costs.

Compare the room hire and catering rates to a 24-hour delegate rate as this can often prove to be more cost effective overall. Is a deposit required and, if so, how much and how far in advance? What's the cancellation policy should take up be lower than expected and will you receive a full or partial refund? If it's an exhibition you're booking, will you get a discount if you opt for multiple events? Don't forget to use your negotiation skills. Many quoted costs are open for discussion.

Turn up, enjoy and follow-up

After all your efforts, relax and enjoy. But it doesn't end when you've said goodbye to the last stragglers. Plan follow-up activity in the form of thank you emails to your attendees for being there on the day, seeking their feedback in a survey, giving presentation slides or key takeaways from speakers and gently reminding them of your next scheduled event. Try to cement your relationship by offering other calls to action (i.e. sign up to your monthly e-newsletter). For non-attendees, refine your content for a "sorry you couldn't attend" email. This may be an opportune time to inform them about future similar events you're hosting or offering other means of meeting up and entering into discussion.

If you set your objectives at the outset, it's time to measure how well you've achieved them afterwards using ROI metrics.

Webinars

In the legal profession, face-to-face meetings have traditionally been used for networking purposes. However, in the fast-paced, hectic modern workplace, this isn't always possible. With a combination of audio, video and application sharing, webinars are the next best thing to direct physical contact. We would argue, better, because of the time and financial savings which can be achieved in the process. Not least by attendees themselves who can participate from the comfort and convenience of their own desk.

With webinars, you can literally connect and communicate with many individuals simultaneously (even those in the provinces), mixing together verbal presentations with PowerPoint slides, showing documents or features in various applications, asking questions or holding polls (surveys) for immediate electronic response whilst appearing via webcam on attendees' screens.

Technology is constantly changing so embrace webinar technology and use to your commercial advantage. Our webinar tips are:-

Familiarise yourself and test beforehand

Whether you're using an in-house or external webinar hosting solution, familiarise yourself before the live event. Set up dummy webinars with colleagues as attendees then rehearse the proper webinar with your speakers.

Once you're confident, confirm your webinar title and content, book your speakers, set up PowerPoint presentations and invite people to attend. Use the handy hints from our earlier 'Events' section.

Define your attendees and their roles

"The more, the merrier" doesn't always apply to meetings, virtual or otherwise, unless of course it's a prospecting exercise. Some people could instead watch the recording in their own time or read notes distributed post webinar.

Pre-assign five key roles for the webinar: leader, facilitator, knowledge manager, gatekeeper and technologist. The purpose of attendees should be clear thus setting their expectations as to their expected level of participation.

Get ready early

Log in around half an hour prior to kick off so that any technical hitches can be resolved before attendees arrive. Check the audio and slides, get ready for your speakers to join, and finally your registrants.

Set some general housekeeping ground rules

To fully engage with attendees, you want to stop them (where possible) from multi-tasking and being distracted from your webinar. Ask them (politely) to switch off emails, mobile phones (unless they're being used to listen in to the webinar) and clear away paperwork from their viewing place.

You may wish to request use of the mute button. Someone coughing or tapping away on their keyboard (or worse, yawning!) in the background is very distracting.

If attendees need to temporarily step away (it's occasionally inevitable), ask them to switch to offline status and return to online when they're back. Otherwise, you could be left wondering why they're not responding to directly addressed questions.

To allow sufficient time for logging on, set registration as 5 minutes earlier, so that when the time comes to start your meeting, you're not still waiting for people to arrive. Your attendees will appreciate your punctuality if you begin on time.

Understand your meeting objectives and circulate an agenda

Objectives need to be understood not just by you, but also your meeting attendees. Why are you holding the webinar? To share inform-ation, inform decision making, evaluate options, generate ideas, demonstrate expertise, solve a problem or another reason?

An agenda serves three purposes: acts as a reference against which to prepare beforehand; provides a script for the meeting, and a mechanism for control and order; and represents a standard by which the meeting can be judged. You'd distribute an agenda for face-to-face meetings; webinars should be no different. Also, an agenda can incentivise people to attend. So make your agenda interesting.

Use compelling content to keep your audience engaged

Your attendees have busy lives and don't have time to waste listening to your spiel about your organisation's greatness! A webinar shouldn't just be an online version of your standard sales pitch. Make attendance worth their while by addressing their needs, issues, fears and wants; not talking in length about your service offerings.

Record for future use

If you have the ability, record the webinar during the live broadcast. You can use this later either to send out to non-attendees or enhance your marketing campaigns. All you'd need is a hyperlink to the recorded webinar to keep plugging the same message and achieve higher return on your efforts.

Remember your follow-up exercises

So, your webinar's gone swimmingly. But don't forget your follow ups. Just as for live events, send out your "thank you" and "sorry you couldn't attend" emails. Provide minutes, action items and even the recording to relevant individuals.

Directories

As you know, October heralds the publication of the legal guides and you find out the rankings of your individual solicitors, barristers, overall practice or chambers in specific areas of expertise.

The directories are used, as you might expect, to back-up the marketing activities which you're already doing. Once a company or individual has a specific matter, they'll look to the directories for guidance, particularly when there's little else to differentiate one legal service provider from another. A high ranking, therefore, gives you the edge.

So what is it that the directories measure and how do they measure it? Well, they typically measure the collective strength of the law firm or barristers' chambers in the practice area, general reputation in the market, number of solicitors or barristers practising in those areas, numbers ranked as leading individuals and their seniority profile. For the solicitors and barristers themselves, they measure the amount and quality of work done in specific areas, complexity / profile of cases handled in the past 12 months, proportion of time spent on work in that area, relevant past experience, credible work highlights, precedent-setting cases and market feedback from solicitors, general counsel and peers.

Research by the directories takes the form of an email sent to listed references and interviews (telephone-based predominantly) conducted with a selection of client referees, be it non-legal companies, solicitors, general counsel or barristers.

Here's what makes a good submission:-

Deadlines met

Hundreds of solicitors and barristers submit entries each year. The result is thousands of references that need to be checked, contacted and responses collated. All that takes time. It's vitally important that you meet the deadlines if everything is to be completed in a timely fashion. The directories themselves warn that they won't accept late submissions.

At the very least, you need to have the referee spreadsheets in on time so they can begin the process of de-duplicating and contacting referees. The reason for this earlier deadline is that any issues in low response rate can be flagged up sooner and dealt with, meaning the response rate from your clients will be more successful and the chances of receiving rankings improves.

Often there is a huge overlap in the referees submitted. In this instance, the directories will send one email to the contact asking for feedback on multiple solicitors, barristers, law firms and barristers' chambers. They don't re-email any contact, therefore if you're late with your spreadsheet and that contact has already been emailed, you've effectively lost your chance at a reference from that person.

Structured submissions

Separate submissions are sent for each practice area. Submissions should be succinct but with the correct level of detail as stipulated by the directories in question. Cases need to be explained in layman's terms because the researchers aren't experts. They need to understand simply and quickly why a case is important and why that solicitor or barrister is the best in their field.

Whilst Legal 500 doesn't provide templates, Chambers and Partners does. Either way, they require very similar information. For barristers' chambers, this is:-

- Feedback on rankings in the current edition

- Practice area overview including:-

  - Key achievements of the set within that practice area in the last 12 months

  - Number of barristers in that practice area

  - Name of the individual who leads that practice area

  - Name of the clerk most closely associated with its management

- List of barristers already ranked by the publication you're working on (by order of year of call)

- List of barristers seeking rankings by that publication (again, ordered by year of call)

- Information on each barrister (in order as above) including:-

  - Year of call / year of silk

  - Introduction to their practice

  - USPs of that barrister – what makes them different? What's their niche expertise? Do they have relevant past experience outside the Bar? Are there landmark cases from the last 12 months? What role did they play? Why was the case important?

  - Work highlights – include up to five noteworthy cases handled in the past year covering these 8 points:-

    - Barrister's role (2 sentences)

    - Dates (and case reference if applicable)

- Opposing counsel

- Instructing law firm (and lawyers)

- Why / how the case is significant such as high profile, complex, unique or commercially important

- Press links

- Confidentiality – is the case confidential or publishable?

  ○ Contact details if follow up's needed – name, position, email address and telephone number

For law firms, the submissions process is more extensive. In addition to the introductory paragraphs / bullet points, feedback on the previous directory edition and contact details, you're also required to provide:-

- Team information – summary of who's involved in the team for each practice area including head, leading individuals, recent arrivals and departures

- Next generation lawyers – senior associates and counsel who make a material difference to the practice's offering

- List of active clients – identify new clients and indicate length of longstanding client relationships

- Work highlights – include up to 10 examples from that calendar year

- Appendix – to be used for listing relevant additional information i.e. other recent / previous work

Strong referees

Referees can be anyone your solicitors or barristers have worked closely with who'll be able to provide a fair evaluation of their skills. They can be direct clients, solicitors, opponents, lay clients, leaders (for juniors) or juniors (for leaders). Solicitors should collate between 10 and 20 referees per practice area; barristers 5 or more.

As already indicated, referees should be sent early on in the process, either uploaded to their website or emailed, depending on the directory. A spreadsheet template can be downloaded from the directory research pages. You mustn't change the format of this sheet because it feeds into software that will automatically email the referees with the correct barrister / set names etc. and automatically collate responses. The auto-generated email asks the referees a small number of questions and gives a 2-week window for them to respond.

Put forward referees you know are more likely to respond and who've worked with the solicitor or barrister within the last 12 months. Greater weight is placed on recent referees / cases. Inform the referees of your intention to use them in your submission. Email them with the name of the researcher who'll contact them for feedback and ensure they under-stand it only takes 2 minutes to respond to the 5 questions asked.

Prepared-for interviews

Interviews can be telephone or face-to-face format. Researchers will contact various employees for feedback on their own practice or set, and also on their peers and general practice ideas as well as current rankings.

Make sure that the interviewee has the submission and current rankings in front of them during the interview. Researchers aim to interview each ranked law firm or set, however if a researcher is very familiar with the party concerned, this may not be deemed necessary.

The top misconceptions / mistakes of directory submissions are:-

- Missing the deadlines for referees

- Missing the practice area deadlines

- Sending in submissions containing rankings of rival publications

- Copying and pasting solicitor and barrister profiles and information straight from websites

- Underestimating the importance of the overview section

- Citing cases without any details of the solicitors' or barristers' involvement

- Sending in improperly named submissions (the directories have their own naming conventions – you must follow these)

- Including too many unranked solicitors and barristers (although this can be a nightmare to manage in house, you really need to try and be realistic; focus on those solicitors and barristers that stand the best chance of success; the fewer unranked solicitors and barristers you submit, the more time the researcher has to spend on them and the more likely you are of success)

- For the Legal 500, including referees in the submissions (as noted already, the referees' spreadsheet should be sent separately)

- Again, for the Legal 500, putting forward barristers for ranking with less than 10 years' call (because it's perceived that they're less able to give comprehensive feedback on their peers)

- Missing new category information (requirements do occasionally change)

If you received the rankings you were hoping for, it's more of the same next year. But don't get complacent. There's always room for improvement so introduce refinements to your submissions and you may even move up a rank or retain top spot. Where directory submissions are concerned, it pays to be a perfectionist!

On the other side of the coin, if you failed to achieve your anticipated status, learn from your mistakes to generate more favourable results next time round. This may mean structuring your submissions differently, writing case details better, selecting stronger referees or preparing carefully for interview.

Cause-related marketing

As well as responsibilities to your clients, employees and other close stakeholders, you have an ethical and environmental duty to your wider community and surroundings.

Going beyond your primary legal duties and actively striving to undertake activities for the furtherance of social and ecological good is better for business because it shows you're concerned about society at large, the world around you and aren't completely profit-obsessed.

Stories about corporate philanthropy are often featured in the news, whether on a regional or national basis, so positive publicity about your corporate social responsibility (CSR) initiatives may secure press coverage for your organisation and help boost your public profile.

Job seekers and prospective clients too consider organisations' engagement in CSR before deciding where to work and who to instruct for their matters. So, it can assist with recruiting the best talent and gaining new clients.

Some companies undertake CSR without a defined programme or team / individual to manage everything. This haphazard approach is less effective than a systematic system fuelled by goals, with defined budgets, timescales and human resource allocations. All of which can be managed and monitored to determine the success of your CSR schemes.

The key question is what to do in order to show your caring side. This is where cause-related marketing comes in. The obvious answer is pro bono services, taking on voluntary casework for individuals or community groups who otherwise can't afford to pay for legal repres-entation.

Another project may be fundraising throughout the year for a main (or multiple) charity(ies). Or perhaps supporting major professionally organised events, be it fundraisers dedicated to the legal industry such as the annual London Legal Support Trust's 10k London Legal Walk or nationwide televised campaigns such as Children in Need, Red Nose Day and Sports Relief.

Following on from this, you could choose a non-profit organisation to form a close connection with. With your joint marketing resources, you can conduct an ongoing series of campaigns, PR amongst them, to raise awareness of your togetherness. Backing a major cause in this way and taking a cooperative stance allows you to generate positive publicity and improve client relations, both of which are good for business.

From a green perspective, you could volunteer for environmental activities or start your own recycling project. It doesn't have to be a massive undertaking. It can be as straightforward as visiting your local park and tidying up litter or collecting shredded paper to take to your regional recycling bank.

Our advice is this – allow your employees to be an active part of the brainstorming and decision-making stages. Enlist customers' support too. You'll get everyone on board and identify opportunities you may never have thought of in a million years. Then go out and show everyone how committed you are to the purpose.

Be wary, though, of the potential mistrust element. Be transparent about how any funds are being generated (i.e. you're not just charging clients more for your services with the excess monies going to the cause) and used (if possible, provide some concrete evidence of how the cause is benefitting from your donations).

Conclusion

This chapter should have illustrated yet more marketing tools with which to promote and, ultimately, sell your wares. Standalone, they can help you reach whole new target markets for your services. Integrated, they have the combined power to really drive your audience into action.

Whilst advertising, advertorials and events cost money, press releases, webinars, directories and cause-related marketing are free, other than the cost of your own time. So, where you're able to save in one area, invest in another, to use your marketing budget effectively.

Our closing comments are:-

1. Advertising – blend copy with graphics on the best platforms but don't expect to see instant ROI.

2. Press releases and advertorials – try press releases first; if all else fails, switch to paid-for advertorials for assured coverage of your company news and announcements.

3. Events and webinars – decide if real or virtual is the best fit for the occasion bearing in mind the differing organisational challenges of both types.

4. Directories – go all out to maximise your chances of inclusion / promotion in the legal guides.

5. Cause-related marketing – as well as giving you the feel-good factor, demonstrating your commitment to CSR brings benefits which directly impact your profit margins and recruitment capabilities.

CHAPTER SEVEN
THE IMPORTANCE OF DESIGN

Why do marketers place so much emphasis on design? Well the easy answer is that a good design can communicate your brand, aspirations and messages far easier than a myriad of words. A bad design can do the reverse – very easily!

There are variety of things you will need to include when evaluating your current deigns. Everything from your website, logo and brochures to presentation materials, tender documents and invoices. The key to implementing a good design is understanding where the designs will be used, the medium they will be used on, the ease of message communication and the reflection of your brand values.

Three of the main areas we are often asked about are logos, invitations and the use of stock photography. In this chapter we will look at how to design the perfect logo for your organisation, what to think about when designing event invitations and where you can source imagery that complements your brand. But first we need to discuss design and what elements you will need to consider in all your marketing collateral.

There are ten basic elements of design that you must consider for your collateral, websites and other documentation. Some you may be able to dismiss, but before you do that, you need to understand what they are and how they may be relevant:-

1. Lines – sounds pretty basic, a line is a line. However, the type of line; dotted, dashed, solid etc. can have a visual impact on your overall design piece. You'll also need to consider where you use them, the frequency and consistency across mediums.

2. Typography – this is essential. People have to be able to read what's written. Your font selected says a lot about who you are and how professional your organisation is. Writing in 'Culz MT' or 'Comic Sans' is never a good idea for corporations (or indeed anyone over the age of 6).

3. Colour – we go into more detail on colour wheels below. However, you will need to consider the type of colour, bold or pastel, the placement of colour background or standalone alongside when and where it is to be used. It's also worth noting that the acceptance of colour varies from product to product and market to market. There's a reason blue Kit-Kat wrappers never took off. Very few people find blue food wrappers appealing.

4. Shapes – these are often used to give proportion to a collateral piece. They can be used to communicate more subliminal brand elements too. For example, many forward thinking companies will use ovals or incomplete circles to communicate openness and they will shy away from solid shapes and rigid forms of squares and rectangles. Whilst they can communicate strength, they can also communicate rigidity and inflexibility. Who knew there was so much to a shape?

5. Texture – texture and textured images create interest even on mediums that you don't touch such as websites and blogs. They can convey subliminal messages. For example an image of silk used as a background can convey extravagance. We know what silk feels like and by seeing it our brains have made the connection between the image and the experience.

6. Space – this generally relates to 'negative space' or the blank areas on your collateral or website. Space allows the reader to remain calm and to order their thoughts. How many times have you seen a cluttered document and thought you just can't be bothered reading it? Space can also be used to draw the reader's eye to more important paragraphs or images.

7. Scale – varying the size and shape of objects can add interest and variety for a reader. You do need to be careful though and don't litter the page with random objects of varying sizes for the sake of it. As with everything marketing related, if there's not a proper reason for doing something – don't do it!

8. Equilibrium – asymmetry is eye-catching and designers love it. However, for non-creative people it can be an OCD nightmare. The symmetry (or not) of your communication pieces should reflect your company and your market. There's little point in being all designer and cutting-edge if it's a turn-off for your prospects and clients. This is why test-marketing is crucial.

9. Emphasis – using bold text or italics to emphasise a quote, phrase or point is commonplace. Sadly overusing it is also commonplace. When producing copy, take a step back and un-focus your eyes. If there is too much italicised or bold text, go back and define the points that you really want to make and highlight only these. Your communication piece will be better received for it.

10. Harmony – a great design is a combination of all of the above. It should gel so that the reader doesn't even notice it. It should communicate your message clearly and leave the reader with the feeling that you are easily understood and easy to do business with.

Whilst we're on the subject of layouts and typography, one of the most common mistakes lawyers make when producing copy (for clients in particular) is that they justify the text so that the overall document is uniform. Stop it! Average people (and by that we mean everyone who is not a lawyer) is not used to this format. Even most magazines and newspapers are moving away from this outdated appearance. It's exceptionally difficult to read copy that's written in this way. The words are spaced randomly resulting in 'rivers' of white spaces. These rivers draw the reader's eye and detract from the actual text. Everything you produce should be easy to read and easy to respond to, otherwise you risk making your clients feel like you're hard work and they just won't bother with you. The only exception to the 'justification sin' is books (as you'll have noticed), where publishing houses still insist on full justification of the text.

In this chapter on all-things design related, read about:-

- How to design the perfect logo

- Invitation designs

- The importance of images

How to design the perfect logo

When it comes to logos, some companies are undisputed crown bearers. This visual aspect of these logo heavyweights' brand identity is universally recognised. For example, think about Apple's bitten apple or Wikipedia's jigsaw-puzzle globe.

However, champions of the logo world don't always use images in their logos. Sometimes, it's the typeface and colours alone that make logos so distinguishable. For instance, consider Coca Cola's easily identifiable red handwriting-font.

Of course, what these brand greats have in common is big marketing budgets. With such ample funds, it's possible to create iconic logos such as these. But, we're here to prove that, even with modest finances, you can still design a knock-out logo.

Here's how…

Be unique

Forget the old saying "imitation is the best form of flattery". With logos, plagiarism is a definite no-no. Be original and, once you have some logo artwork in mind, check it out online to be sure a similar form doesn't already exist elsewhere. You don't want to land yourself in hot water after all your hard designing work. You can check to see if your logo is already being used by visiting https://www.gov.uk/search-for-trademark.

The way to achieve true originality is to brainstorm what your brand means to you and other people in your set / firm. Your logo is, after all, your visual keystone and should reflect your organisation's personality. Researching your clients and prospects is another great way to see how you are currently positioned in the marketplace and what values you are perceived as having. Often there is a huge difference of opinion between what the organisation believes and what the market believes.

Choose a fitting colour scheme

According to psychologists, every colour has a different, significant implication. Orange suggests creativity, friendliness and youthfulness; black oozes credibility and powerfulness; white's all about simplicity and purity; etc.

While it may be tempting to opt for bold colours that stand out from the crowd, this may actually be sending the wrong message about your brand. Your colour scheme should support your messaging, not damage it.

Decide upon wordmark and / or symbol

As stated earlier, your logo may comprise a wordmark and / or symbol. When deciding upon typefaces, avoid gimmicky fonts as these often quickly turn out of fashion and can be tricky to read. Helvetica is a simple, well-used logo font. Or, you could maybe use an off-the-shelf font as a starting point and tweak it to your tastes. You must also consider the written version of your company name. Too many designers produce complex fonts that aren't freely available. The result is that your employees will simply use the font that looks closest to the logo, causing a cacophony of typefaces, inconsistency and a huge waste of marketing money.

Your logo should work equally well on paper as on multiple digital devices for both off and online purposes. We can't tell you the number of times that companies have employed designers to come up with the most intricate logos, all of which look beautiful but are completely impractical as they can't transfer onto multiple media or different formats. They turn out to be beautiful white elephants.

Additionally, you should be able to use the logo in part or whole form (with the words and symbol or the symbol alone). This gives you much greater flexibility for placement of the logo. Sadly, too many companies have not thought of this and have been left with a cumbersome logo they are unable to use credibly.

Generate diverse logo formats and usage guidelines

Once you've arrived at your new logo design, produce it in multiple formats and file types including full colour, reverse (for use on dark or photographic backgrounds) and monochrome (grey and black, all-black and all-white) as gif, jpg and pdf images.

Preparing usage guidelines wouldn't go amiss either. This will clearly define things such as colour palettes, minimum sizing, exclusion areas, shaping and backgrounds with examples throughout of both good and bad practice in collateral such as letterheads, compliments slips, business cards, tender documents, PowerPoint presentations and adverts. These will ensure your logo's applied correctly and consistently.

Register your logo and trademarks

You can register your trademark to protect your brand e.g. the name of your product or service. When you register your trademark, you'll be able to: take legal action against anyone who uses your brand without your permission, including counterfeiters; put the ® symbol next to your brand – to show that it's yours and warn others against using it; and sell and license your brand.

You can learn more about registering logos and trademarks at https://www.gov.uk/how-to-register-a-trade-mark/register-a-trade-mark.

Be patient

Your logo won't become iconic overnight. It'll gain popularity slowly and build brand awareness gradually. Launching your new-look logo should be supported by marketing activity. Don't be shy. You've spent time and effort on your artwork so tell everyone about it. It's useful to tell your clients that you are developing your brand. Write to them with the old logo and the new one so they know what to look out for. Take the time to explain why you're embarking on this and how it will move the company forward. If you don't know why you're doing it, maybe that's a good indicator that you should stop. Marketing money should always be spent wisely and spending money that would be used to bring in new instructions on an ego trip is not wise.

Over the years, we've worked at a number of high-profile businesses who felt that in order to obtain the perfect logo they needed to spend a fortune. I've lost count of the number of times I've sat in logo design meetings with some of the UK's biggest agencies only to be presented with re-hashed AT&T logos or logos dragged up from the early 1970s (the designers tend to be younger and therefore don't realise that some of us dinosaurs were around when these logos were used first time round and, furthermore, we remember the disasters they were associated with!).

Invitation designs

The application of a logo is most prominent in invitation designs, however, the invitations themselves can prove rather difficult for some companies to master. When creating invitation designs it's often useful to go back to basics at the start.

First and foremost, before you write a word of the invitation you must have decided on the theme of your event, decided your agenda and your booked venue. Now it's time to write, design and send your invitations.

Put simply, a well-written and nicely designed invitation should make your event impossible to resist. Proper invitation etiquette is demanded in order to avoid missing important details for your delegates and to grab their attention thus enticing them along. Your recipients deserve (and expect) to be informed and inspired by your invitation. Don't disappoint them!

Our 5 top tips will help to keep you on track…

<u>1: Plan ahead</u>

As a rule of thumb, you should allow at least 6-8 weeks before the event for sending out invites. Your recipients have busy professional and social lives, so plenty of notice is advisable. You also need to factor in some time for copywriting, approval, design, printing and posting. Don't get caught short. A last minute rush won't result in the best-ever invitation and a full house! It's worth sending a 'save the date' well in advance of the event if it's likely to be popular or is at a time when many other events are going on. The save the date card can also buy you a bit more time for developing the actual invitation.

<u>2: Vital statistics</u>

This is a balancing act. Provide sufficient information to give guests an insight into why (and how) they should invest their valuable time with you, but keep high level enough so that you don't give too much away. Intrigue will add to the appeal of your event. A basic schedule of speakers, activities and breaks, with registration, start and finish times will do the trick.

It's safest to assume that attendees don't know the venue. Provide full details of the destination including map, driving directions and transport network routes. It should be clear who's inviting them, when it's taking place and other important details such as dress code.

<u>3: RSVP and data capture</u>

A clear call to action is essential otherwise your delegates won't know how to reply, negatively or positively. Depending on the nature of your event and internal resources, this could be something as straightforward as a phone number or email address for a designated chambers clerk to collate, or more sophisticated online electronic registration system for automatic data capture of complicated delegate details such as contact information, dietary requirements, transportation needs etc. It's always useful to give your clients an option for responding, some prefer the electronic options that put the event into their diaries, whilst others are happy to pick up the phone or send an email.

4: Rule of KISS

We may sound like we're contradicting ourselves here, but overcrowding your invitation can be off-putting, as your recipients will feel overwhelmed with the volume of information you're bombarding them with. So, once written, read back through your invite and see if there's anything that can be edited out. In the marketing world, we love acronyms, and this one's known as the KISS rule (Keep It Simple Stupid!).

5: Eye-catching design

Despite any protestations to the contrary, we all 'judge a book by its cover'. Whether you're opting for paper or electronic format (this decision may be down to recipients' communication preferences or your budget restrictions), imagine that you only have a few seconds to attract attention. Think about strong images, typography, paper stock, printing techniques and database accuracy (you don't want letters addressed to Mrs Stephen Surname Not Known!). Your recipients will notice the effort (or lack of it!).

The importance of images

Imagery is an important part of marketing. An image can covey a 1,000 words as the saying goes, however, you need to make sure that the 1,000 words the image is conveying is actually what you want it to say and that it reflects your brand and business.

Sometimes we see images and wonder what relevance they have to the text. At these times we spend more time thinking about that than actually reading and digesting the text. We suspect that this wasn't the outcome the company was wanting when they spent their marketing money on that piece of collateral!

Further to the importance of the image fitting the communication piece, it's also imperative that you have the rights to use the image in your work.

It's so easy to find images for your on- or off-line marketing campaigns on the internet. A quick Google Images search, right click, save and you're done. But is it legal? The unequivocal answer is 'no'!

Image copyright ownership is a complex issue. Use an image without permission and you could face a hefty fine. Suddenly the 'free' image has just cost you hundreds (if not thousands) of pounds and caused huge embarrassment on your part.

Well-known image libraries are aplenty where you can buy stock images for anything from circa £5 to £500. We would suggest a look at sites such as deposit photos (http://depositphotos.com) or Fotolia (www.fotolia.com) where the images are reasonably priced and the search facilities mean that you can quickly find the type of images you are looking for.

Again, you need to think about how you intend to use the image and how it may be reproduced in different formats or on different mediums. Isolated images (those without backgrounds) are probably the most versatile. The higher the resolution the better and the more flexibility you have in reproduction.

But isn't it nice to get some things for free? There are a few free stock photo sites so you can bring your campaigns to life without it costing you the earth. We would suggest that you take a look at the following sites:-

1. Pexels (https://www.pexels.com/)

This site promises 10,000 free stock photos and 3,000 new high resolution photos added each month. It uses the Creative Commons Zero (CC0) licence. Images are supplied by its community of photographers and other legitimate sources.

2. Life of Pix (http://www.lifeofpix.com/)

These high resolution photos are readily available within the public domain on an unrestricted basis for commercial and personal use. Again, it relies upon a network of photographers to build its library and the CC0 licence applies. The library is fairly limited though.

3. Death to the Stock Photo (http://deathtothestockphoto.com/)

On this platform, you can sign up to receive free monthly image packs by email. There is a slight catch in that you can pay for premium membership in order to access an extended library of photos. It's subject to 'Photograph End User Licence' and 'Terms of Service'.

4. Unsplash (https://unsplash.com/)

This site's owners invite photographers to upload new photos which is how they build their stocks. Promises unlimited use on a CC0 licence basis.

5. Picjumbo (https://picjumbo.com/)

Useable for free but some terms apply. Premium membership gives access to 1000+ extra images within its premium collection (over and above what's available for free) and 30+ new photos every month. Images are nicely categorised to simplify searching.

6. Gratisography (http://gratisography.com/)

More of the same. Easily downloadable photos with new images added weekly. CC0 licence applies.

A word of caution, however, is still advised. The CC0s of these sites vary significantly. You will need to check the small print to avoid any possibility of infringement.

Conclusion

What to take away from this chapter:-

1. A good design can communicate your brand, aspirations and messages far easier than a myriad of words. A bad design can do the reverse – very easily!

2. With logos, plagiarism is a definite no-no (to be fair, plagiarism is never a good thing). You need to be original and then check to make sure that noone else is using it.

3. Your logo is your visual keystone and should reflect your organisation's personality.

4. Brainstorm in your organisation and consult clients for feedback on your brand to ensure you are perceived how you want to be.

5. Your colour scheme should support your messaging, not damage it.

6. Keep in mind that logos are used across many different mediums, they have to appear the same on everything or the inconsistency will damage your brand value.

7. You must register your logo and trademark to ensure your brand is protected.

8. Invitations should be clean, easy to read and informative.

9. Invitations should also be easy to respond to.

10. Think about strong images, typography, paper stock, printing techniques and database accuracy for your invitations to reflect your business and event accurately and elicit a positive response.

11. It's important for any image used to fit the communication piece. It must be relevant.

12. It's also imperative that you have the rights to use the image in your work. Ensure you comply with the terms and conditions.

CHAPTER EIGHT
DEVELOPING CLIENTS AND
ACQUIRING PROSPECTS

As service providers, in order to succeed, law firms and chambers must deliver quality services. This applies to both your employees / clerks' room and fee earners, partners or barristers managing instructions and legal cases respectively.

A mediocre standard of service is no longer acceptable (and never should have been!). Clients' expectations are higher than they've ever been and competition's never been tougher. Offer poor service standards and your clients will take their next instruction elsewhere. Your competitors will be more than happy to welcome them into their organisation.

Let's elaborate a moment. It's time for your haircut. You walk into your hairdressing salon. No one greets you at the reception desk or offers you a drink. You sit yourself down but there are no magazines to browse while you wait your turn. Eventually, your hairdresser's ready to do your hair. He / she doesn't smile or chat, other than the perfunctory "come and sit here" at the beginning and "does that look okay?" at the end. Even if your hair looks amazing and the price was low, the distinctly underwhelming experience will probably deter you from going again.

It's just the same in firms / chambers. Treat your clients well and they'll return time and time again, becoming regular users of your services. After you've gone to the effort and expense of securing them in the first place (it's readily acknowledged that the cost of acquiring new clients far exceeds the cost of retaining them thereafter), it's in your best interests to do your utmost to keep them.

In order to deliver great customer care and build long-lasting relationships with your client base, you should:-

Understand clients' real needs

This may necessitate interviewing, surveying or benchmarking activities to find out what clients seek in their interactions with you, and ascertain current perceptions of your organisation compared to the competition.

Tailor your services accordingly

This could involve extending your specialisms, opening for longer hours, reviewing your pricing options (ie. fixed fees and packages), assessing your readiness for direct access and considering online service delivery.

Establish rich and frequent client contact

Whatever your recipients' preferences – email, post or in-person – set up regular communications so that they feel valued and stay close to you. Hard copy mailers, email newsletters, industry event attendance, social media posts, blog entries, face-to-face meetings and occasional phone calls will form part of your communication toolkit.

Make customer satisfaction the responsibility of every member of your organisation

This item's a little trickier to address. It may require creating policy documents for best practice and adopting templates or frameworks for correspondence. These measures – and more besides – will ensure each and every interaction with your clients is the absolute best it can be. Internal marketing can be a challenge as you're effectively trying to change the mindset of the majority of people. Treat your staff well and invest time in training them on the importance of client care, and you'll turn them into your frontline brand ambassadors.

<u>Consider how you deal with complaints</u>

With social media giving people a powerful, wide-reaching voice, it's vital to approach complaints sensitively, otherwise the whole world will know about your poor service in an instant. Listen, gather facts, escalate the issue (if necessary) and come to a mutually agreeable resolution. Often, complaining clients go on to become advocates, if the situation's dealt with appropriately.

By tackling these areas, your firm or chambers can become client centric with client service your primary focus. To help you really grasp this concept and learn how to change your ethos, read about the following in this chapter:-

- Putting the client at the heart of the business

- The DOs and DON'Ts of customer profiling

- Market research and surveys

- Leveraging your existing clients

- Converting promoters into case studies

Putting the client at the heart of the business

'Client centric' and 'customer focused' are terms often bandied around in marketing circles, but what exactly does it mean? Quite simply, it's about concentrating first-and-foremost on meeting clients' needs, whatever it takes. And yes, the customer is always right!

When you've gone to the huge effort of winning new clients (remember the rule: it costs five times more to acquire than to retain clients!), it's vital you do your utmost to keep them. Otherwise, your hard-earned clients will take their business elsewhere. I'm pretty sure your competitors will welcome them with open arms!

Of course, it's unrealistic to expect every client to remain loyal, even if the service they receive from your firm / chambers is of high quality, but it'll certainly improve your chances.

So, what's the key to great client service? These are the requirements of your client base:-

- Speed, clarity and understanding – quick resolution, options with projected outcomes and jargon-free language are what's needed here. Clearly not every case can be quickly resolved. However, setting and updating client expectations and interpreting those for lay clients if appropriate will go a long way to building trust and avoiding any unnecessary shocks that can result in negative opinions and feedback.

- Approachability and trust – being friendly, open, personable and honest will build long-term professional relationships. These skills are increasingly important as 'people buy from people' and whilst one barrister for example might be the best in the business, if they are rude to clients or unapproachable, they cease to be an attractive purchase and a less skilled but more approachable barrister will win the instruction.

- Availability and responsiveness – regular communications, sometimes outside of normal working hours where cases necessitate extra flexibility and prompt replies to queries show you're willing to go the extra mile. These qualities are great differentiators too, particularly in areas of law that are more commodity driven.

- Value and price – value-added support through proactive actions, and transparent and competitive pricing means that your services are worth every penny. Notice how we haven't said that you must offer low pricing. That's because 'value' is in the eye of the beholder. One person may place a higher value on you being readily available and able to communicate directly with lay-clients than another and is thus happy to pay a higher premium for that extra service.

Before you start implementing changes to client care in order to raise standards, you need to know what clients, lapsed clients and prospective clients think about your organisation and staff. In order to attain this knowledge, you will need to survey clients, prospects and ex-clients. Rather than being a one-off exercise, the surveys need to be a repeated programme, each time using the feedback gained to resolve any substandard aspects of your services. That way, you'll keep going from strength to strength.

Market research and surveys

As we have already established, client service should be at the heart of everything you do. Quality service delivery secures the future of your business and should be a process of continual refinement. With proper insight into your reputation, perceived performance and comparison with other sets, you can make real improvements to the way you operate and conduct your law firm / chambers.

People buy from people and consumers of legal services are no different from anyone else. Clients prefer to instruct counsel whom they find approachable, trustworthy and responsive, and potentially with whom they can build long-term relationships with, at a competitive price. This is what good client service is all about – value for money.

To understand perceptions of your organisation, and to compare how you stand in the marketplace, it is best to use a mix of surveys and market research. The results can be enlightening... how you perceive yourself, and how others perceive you, are often poles apart.

It's also worth noting that respondees are more forthcoming and honest in their answers when dealing with an outside agency rather than directly with you as they're less afraid of offending you.

NPS: A single number; multiple insights

There is often a discrepancy between lawyers' and end clients' opinions on the quality of their services. The only way to truly gauge what your clients think about you is by asking them. And it's only by finding out what they really think that you are able to improve your service offerings.

Measuring service effectiveness could take the form of in-depth satisfaction surveys, one-to-one interviews and focus group discussions. Another increasingly popular method is Net Promoter Score (NPS) surveys.

NPS is a straightforward metric which has gained popularity thanks to its simplicity. Here's how it works…

The NPS process

To undertake an NPS survey, you (via a third party ideally) should contact all your clients, past and present, with an initial brief survey asking two basic questions:-

1. Would you recommend our organisation to a friend or colleague?

2. How would you suggest we improve our services to you?

As there are only two questions, responding couldn't be easier leading to greater response rates than with traditional research methods. Survey participants rate on a scale of 0 to 10. Depending on where they're positioned on the scale, they're then divided into three groupings:-

Promoters (score 9-10) are loyal enthusiasts who will continue buying and will refer others, fuelling new business development.

Passives (score 7-8) are satisfied but unenthusiastic customers who might be receptive to competitive offerings.

Detractors (score 0-6) are unhappy customers who can damage your brand and impede growth through negative word of mouth.

Obviously, a high rating is the objective! To calculate your overall NPS, subtract the percentage of detractors from the percentage of promoters.

Typically, organisations with the highest customer loyalty (or NPS score) increase revenues at more than twice the rate of competitors who've achieved lower ratings. However, just knowing your NPS score isn't enough. You need to understand how your findings can help you improve your offerings.

Building on your NPS results

Alongside the NPS questions, you should also be exploring additional market benchmark criteria including the amount of time clients have used legal services this year compared to last, and if they predict that this will increase or not in the coming years. You should also seek out trends such as decreased external spend and detect buyer behaviour patterns. Finally, any client research should examine the primary criteria used when hiring counsel and also when not hiring counsel.

Identifying how a firm / set compares in relation to others is vitally important in order to realise over or under-performance. Clients are fairly forthcoming in survey responses, particularly if they can see that their opinions are valued and will lead to improvements, as this will directly impact upon the services they receive in the future. Questions should examine the quality of advice given, approachability of the team involved, resourcefulness of the admin / clerks' room and how you can enhance the client experience, amongst others.

Interpreting your NPS data

With a representative number of responses, you can interpret the data to garner current perceptions, weaknesses for improvement and formulate long-term plans which place clients at the heart of your business.

These plans should include ongoing communications with clients to make them feel they've played a part in improving the services they receive. Tell them about the services to be improved, how they will be improved and, finally, how they have been improved.

In short, the changes introduced by firms / chambers, provided they are properly communicated, lead to increased client retention, increased instructions and increased turnover, all of which have a positive effect on profitability.

NPS as an ongoing process

A one-off survey won't suffice. Taking regular snapshots of service levels and clients' opinions is essential if you're to keep your improvement programme on track and maintain competitive advantage.

It's also worth mentioning that when you do have clients who are avid promoters, you need to be using them to deliver more than just a directory or website quote! Work with that client to network through other departments in their company. You may also have an opportunity to work with their clients; adding value for both of you in their client's eyes by presenting a 'team' solution to their issues.

The closer the links you have with your promoters, the more you will grow your business. It will also have the added benefit of making life very difficult for your competition to get a foothold.

Leveraging your existing clients

Talking of foothold, one of the most common complaints from legal services providers is that their clients only use them for some matters and not for others that are also within their specialism.

In order to address this you need to ask an important question … "*do our clients actually know what else we do*"? All too often they don't know. They come to you with a specific problem, they see the relevant person and then, once the problem is resolved they go again, often having never seen anyone else from the organisation, and depending on what your office facilities are like, they may never have seen any relevant cross branding.

Now, we're not suggesting for one minute that you turn yourselves into Tesco with branding and advertising on every available surface. However, you can make them aware of what you do without looking tacky or desperate for additional business.

A simple selection of brochures which outline the various services you can provide and a file of recent press articles or case updates can make all the difference. Let's face it, clients need something to do whilst they're in reception waiting, they might as well take a look at the full suite of services, with accompanying reference sites, you can offer.

Proactively updating the client regarding their matter instead of being chased by them makes you look professional and seem truly interested in their case. Likewise offering them complementary legal services at a preferential rate is also a good idea. Many of us repeat buy, both on a professional and personal level, from people we like and trust, so these actions, coupled with a prior knowledge of your other services means that when they are in the market for other legal services, you will be their first choice.

There certainly will be more work out there from your existing clients, it's just a matter of ensuring your customer service is top notch and they understand what it is you can do for them and the benefits that you can deliver.

Practical ways of asking for more work (without resorting to clinging to the legs of clients as they leave the building) include: sending emails to your key clients at times when you know you are going to have less work on, telling them that you will be able to turn around papers a little faster than usual. Providing guides to "drafting instructions" which are in effect templates they can fill in (all of which have your details embedded in them). In today's busy legal market, most people will opt for the easy option for time saving reasons, so if you can be as helpful to them as possible, it becomes a "no brainer" for them to fill these in and instruct you for new work. Finally, becoming an authority in a given area and then publishing case updates and relevant news stories to target clients is also a way to maintain the brand awareness and keep your business in their thought process. Regular relevant communication helps to build relationships which inevitably convert into work.

Converting promoters into case studies

So, you've identified happy clients via your NPS survey, directory, website references or other means. Next, you need to convert these into case studies to grow your marketing collateral and give prospective future clients a compelling reason to instruct you.

A healthy library of testimonials speaks volumes about the quality of your services and often is more effective than the best-written marketing campaign simply because they're more believable.

But, if you've never written a case study before, you may be slightly daunted by the whole process, which is why we've devised a handy 5 top tips guide.

1: Tell the story from start to finish

A good case study is a bit like a detective story with a puzzle to be solved. Provide some background to the company / individual who's the protagonist in the case study, introduce the problem, present the solution, outline the benefits and summarise in a conclusion.

You'll also want to include information about your organisation and contact details to get in touch, should your case study inspire your reader to do so.

2: Include real numbers

Vague statements are ambiguous and misleading. Use real figures to make your case study as clear as glass. That way, your reader can visualise where the client began and where they ended, as a direct result of instructing your services. And back it up with evidence in the form of credible quotes from your client. Avoid too much marketing flair! The more realistic they are, the better.

3: Use easy-to-read formatting

Your case study may be riveting, but presented as huge chunks of text will put your readers off. Just as you'd set out other documents, ensure you include headers, sub headers, images, bulleted lists, bold and italicised text. Not only will these formatting elements cater for readers' preferences (namely, skim readers), if you post on your website, it'll boost your SEO rankings too.

4: Sample different structures

People like stories and a uniform structure is nice for familiarity, however, sometimes it's good to break the mould and try something new. Simply set the document out in interview style instead. The sentiments remain the same but, comprising entirely of quotes, it's more credible too.

5: Make them easy to find

Now you've written a knock-out case study, can your target readership find them? Post on your website, share on social media, submit as a press release to legal publications, attach to your marketing campaigns, distribute at events… anything to get noticed.

By truly understanding your clients and prospects you can organise your business in such a way that client centricity becomes the norm. Everyone within the business works for the success of the client and does their best to provide the best possible service. The client feels loved and appreciated, and now has additional knowledge regarding your other services. Repeat instructions and references become more frequent and as a result profits increase. A win-win for everyone!

Conclusion

Takeaways from this chapter are:-

1. Understand clients' real needs and tailor your services accordingly.

2. Establish rich and frequent client contact.

3. Make customer satisfaction the responsibility of every member of your organisation.

4. Consider how you deal with complaints, take action speedily and if you secure a happy outcome, maximise it through additional work or references.

5. Use segmentation and customer profiling to generate personas to help with marketing.

6. Use NPS to understand what you do well and where you can improve.

7. Cross-sell services to existing clients.

8. Leverage existing clients to gain more work or access to new departments.

9. Create case studies to prove that you are very good at what you do and publicise them.

CHAPTER NINE
MANAGING MARKETING
BUDGETS

Setting a marketing budget can be a long and arduous process given the varied ideas partners and members hold about the value of marketing and indeed what actually constitutes marketing. In some organisations the budgeting process consists of thinking of the number of events they plan on holding and adding in a bit of press / PR, maybe some website upgrades and some client entertainment. Not many firms or chambers give any thought to how they are going to quantify the return on their marketing investment or how they should really go about budgeting their marketing investment.

Firstly, everyone needs to understand that marketing is NOT a corporate overhead, it's a necessity not a luxury, it's a financial investment that needs to generate a return that can be measured and monitored. That's easier said than done! Marketing by its nature can be quite difficult to measure. There are so many activities that constitute a campaign. Some activities are shared across campaigns whilst others are very specific. Add in the time and sheer number of touch points it takes to generate a lead and you can be looking at a tracking nightmare.

The nightmare is worth persevering with as it will allow you to really understand what is working and what isn't. Furthermore, the more you can actually show the benefits of marketing, the more you gain the confidence of your set / firm, the more they are likely to invest the following year. So, how much are you currently spending on marketing and is it enough?

According to a recent Council of Chief Marketing Officers report, the answer is no. Most companies are not spending enough to achieve their goals. Their survey shows that 58% of marketing budgets fall below the 4% of revenue mark (a few years ago the average spend was 6% of revenue).

It doesn't make for good reading. But how much control do you have over the budget setting? The answer varies from set to set and firm to firm. Some will have specific budget figures handed down, some will have percentage of projected or past revenue and others may be asked to submit proposals. All will require a marketing plan to set out where the marketing investment is going and all plans should have return on investment projections against them. Whether your budget is handed down or you have a proactive role in determining it, you will need to start with the marketing plan. Once you understand the goals and strategy you will be better placed to formulate a plan and prioritise the budget.

In this chapter, access tips on:-

- Understanding a marketing budget

- How budgets and spends should be determined

- Budget setting and marketing measurement advice

- Five top tips for marketing metrics

Understanding a marketing budget

Whenever your year-end approaches, you, like all other businesses, will be focused on planning for the next financial year, setting budgets and formulating the plans that will enable your business to grow. The overall budget setting for the organisation will also include your marketing budget.

Your marketing budget forms an integral part of your marketing plan, allocating monies to all of your proposed activities, for example campaigns, advertising, events and PR. Without a solid budget, you can easily accidentally overspend on marketing costs so it's a control mechanism. Similarly, you can underspend which may have a disastrous impact on your revenues.

Upon each task's completion, you should log the actual expenditure and compare against your budget. Your budget predominantly acts to forecast and control costs so that you don't excessively overspend, and gives you the ability to analyse performance (specifically return on investment) on your marketing plan's components.

The ability to clearly demonstrate your marketing return on investment to partners and other stakeholders will aid you enormously at the annual resource allocation 'bun-fight' that is the budget setting process. By taking a logical approach to marketing, backed-up with hard facts you can justify any requests for increased investment.

Three usual methods of budget setting

There are three main budgetary processes to consider. They are not mutually exclusive. They are top down, bottom up and projected ROI.

Top down

The top down approach is literally that. It's when you have been handed a figure from on high and you are expected then to allocate spend over the months. It's important not to just evenly distribute spend over the months or you will lead to problems of cash flow later in the year. Instead you must take into account seasonality. Spend will be reduced over the legal holidays for example, or better still, some spend can be reserved for then to bring in additional help for data house-keeping. Spend will be increased around CPD year end when the number of events you hold is likely to increase.

If you are going for a top down approach, we would recommend that your marketing management committee establish a marketing investment figure based on a percentage of revenue as your top down budgetary number. This way marketing is more aligned with the firm's / set's revenue goals and prevents the marketing budget from being some arbitrary number that can be decreased at a whim. As a guideline, the CMO survey shows that 16% of companies spend between 5-6% of revenue on marketing and over 23% spend over 6%. If you are launching a new product or intend to establish your set / firm in a new market, then your spend needs to be in the region of 20% as the amount of activity required to establish yourselves will be far greater than in areas where you are known and respected.

The percentage guideline for a top down approach is 8-10% of revenue, 5% of which is for labour costs (be that staff, outsourcing or a mixture of both). The percentage is determined by a number of factors; how mature the market is, how much education you need to do, how well known your organisation is, how much brand awareness you need to do and finally how fast you intend to grow. Once you have received your top down figure, you then need to calculate your monthly budget figure.

Bottom up

The bottom up approach, as you might expect, is the opposite of the top down approach. This is where you take a look at all the activities you need to do in the year. Take into account the frequency of activities and the constituent parts of campaigns. Segment them into key categories for reporting such as brand materials, press and PR, web and social media, direct mail / email and events. Add activities under each heading and apportion cost estimates. Once you have a "true" cost for all your proposed programmes you can start the budget negotiations with the management team.

Projected ROI

The final method is projected ROI. At the end of the day confidence will grow in marketing when the return on the marketing investment can be clearly demonstrated. The problem with marketing is that it can take a very long time to convert interest into action, particularly when you have a new product or are entering a new market. However, there are some techniques that can be used to validate your marketing plan before you implement it. The same techniques can be used to measure success during and after execution. You will need to compile a set of key assumptions in a return on investment calculator.

The return on investment calculator is basically a spreadsheet of conversion ratios. For example a direct mail piece generally generates a 4% response rate. Telemarketing can generate 20%. The conversion rate of an enquiry to an instruction is 50%. You calculate in the cost of a case type against the income that case type can deliver on average and you can ascertain your return on investment.

This method is useful when looking at niche areas of law where you've only done a limited amount of work but want to expand. You know what you generate from clients in that area already and you have a good feel for the cost of the work done. You knew how many enquiries you had before any instruction was given and so you can therefore estimate revenue based on marketing generated leads.

How budgets and spends should be determined

As we've said, a marketing budget is effectively your marketing plan written in terms of costs based on your estimates as to the 'spend' required to promote your organisation's services to achieve your defined objectives.

However, as we know, budgeting's not an easy task. With such an important role to play in your success, you can't afford to get it wrong. There are three essential steps to help you organise current finances, determine where to spend marketing pounds and make strategic adjustments throughout the year.

Step 1: Organise your financial information

Get organised about your current financial situation. When you're working around estimates, it's impossible to create a realistic marketing budget. Thus, you need real information to work from.

Understanding your finances starts with your revenue information. You need to know how much money your firm / chambers makes on a monthly basis and the variations that might exist. Although income can vary significantly month-by-month, you must use reliable revenue. This is the minimum amount your organisation earns each month. Anything over this monthly minimum is extra revenue that cannot be added to the budget because it's changeable.

A key to understanding your revenue is to understand what types of cases make up the monthly income. You may find that there are a number of common work types each month; for example, you may regularly generate a certain number of conveyancing matters along with a number of wills, a few divorces and a couple of dispute resolution matters. Once you have an idea of where the revenue is coming from you can get a better understanding of how to generate more of it. Obviously if you are regularly dealing with long-duration cases generating vast revenues, you will need to take a view back over a number of years to work out the average revenue in the year, what the cases were that delivered that revenue, and what the likelihood is of more being generated.

You need to have a clear understanding of the market you operate in and what outside influences there may be on the horizon. Changes in legislation could provide new revenue streams for you assuming that you have the necessary skills to deal with those legal challenges in-house. If the revenue stream has enough potential, it may be worth expanding the practice to meet the potential demand.

Once you have an idea of your revenue streams you will need to subtract your business expenses. This includes everything from office space rental to staff salaries. Monthly expenses should be subtracted from the revenue figure before defining your marketing budget. A realistic budget plan will always focus on income that exceeds expenses, not just total revenue.

It's also useful to have an understanding of work-type profitability. How long does it take to complete a case, what level of staff are involved (and their associated costs)? You may find that by analysing this properly you can start to see where the business should be moving and which less-profitable work-type you should be reducing (although sometimes loss leaders are necessary for generating larger incomes).

When you've determined disposable income available for your organisation, decide where this money will be spent. Marketing is only one business area so divide the money based on your strategic goals, of which marketing should form a key part.

Step 2: Decide where to spend marketing monies

Once you know the total amount potentially available for marketing, decide how you intend to spend the money. If you have a limited budget, then you should consider lower-cost activities such as small print adverts, social media and email marketing. With a larger budget, you can afford some events, sponsorship, ambient advertising, printed newsletters and more.

Integral to this stage is reviewing which activities have worked in the past. If email newsletters do the trick, then you should continue, even if you have the funds for more expensive alternatives. Also, consider which channels allow you to reach the right audience. This comes down to customer profiling and finding out where your clients and prospects 'hang out'. It's vital that you build an understanding of where your work is generated as well as which work types are most profitable. From here you can decide which parts of the business you want to focus your resources on to maximum effect.

When considering a new marketing channel, you should set aside some funds for testing. Since you don't know if it'll work for your firm / set, you should only use a small portion of your budget. Once it's tried and tested, invest a little more.

Step 3: Assess data and make appropriate changes

The final step to build a solid marketing budget is analysing the plan and making adjustments which impact positively on revenue. Ultimately, marketing is designed to achieve more revenue. If any of your activities don't do this, then it's better to remove and try something else or invest in proven activities.

Evaluation's the process of comparing performance and recording changes to revenue – has it increased, decreased or stayed the same and can you attribute to any particular marketing activities?

Always keep the budget in mind when you make decisions on marketing spending. That way, you can explore different ideas and find the best marketing mix for your business.

It's important to note that firms and sets are becoming much more commercial enterprises in response to competitive new entrants. Do your budgeting effectively and you can keep up with (or overtake) your competitors in your fight for market share.

Budget setting and marketing measurement advice

Whatever method you adopt for your budgeting process, there are some important questions you need to ask yourself (and your marketing team) to decide how much money to allocate to your planned marketing activities.

These questions relate to key marketing metrics which you should be using in order to measure the success (or, conversely, failure) of the components in your marketing plan. Without detailed analysis of your campaigns and events, you're unable to quantify the best and worst exercises, and you may not be investing in those which deliver the highest return on investment for your law firm / chambers.

Management boards are focused on business growth so you need to present your marketing results in statistical format to the executive team to show the impact of marketing activity on profit, demonstrate the value of budget allocation to marketing and generally get yourself taken seriously as a marketer.

Here are the fundamental questions to guide your measurement insight…

1. What are your SMART (specific, measurable, achievable, realistic and timed) objectives for marketing investment and how will you connect your investments to incremental revenue and profit?

2. What impact would a 10% change in your marketing budget (up or down) have on your profits and margins over the next year? What about the next 3 years?

3. Compared to relevant benchmarks for your firm / chambers (historical, competitive, marketplace), how effective are you at converting marketing investment directly into revenue and profit growth?

4. Which are the appropriate targets for improving revenue leverage (that is, pounds of profit over pounds of marketing and sales spend) over the next few years? Which marketing initiatives will get you there?

5. What questions do you still need to answer with regard to your knowledge of the return on marketing investments? What are you going to do to answer them?

Five top tips for marketing metrics

Now that you've set your marketing budget for the coming year, how do you know with any certainty what each pound spent on marketing brings back in new instructions?

The answer is through marketing metrics. You need to conquer the data with key analytics and turn the information into insights and outcomes. Growth through marketing can only truly be understood via effective analytics.

But, where to begin? Here are five top tips to get you started…

1. Maintaining consistency and alignment

Be sure that your measurement decisions are consistent with your organisation's established business plan. Align the two (metrics and strategy) for best success. There's no point in measuring something that has no relevance, it just wastes time and resources.

2. Starting small

Select one marketing tactic to measure, apply the metric and see how it works for you. Then refine the metric based on what you learn. Meanwhile, select an additional tactic to measure. And so on. You can keep building your measurement programme reasonably and gradually, until eventually you're productively measuring every tactic.

3. Selecting your first tactic to measure

If you're unsure which tactic to select as your first, either choose an easy or important tactic to measure. Some tactics are easy, some are impossible or nearly impossible, and most are somewhere in between. You can gain experience and confidence more quickly if you start with an easier challenge, hence why to choose the former.

The latter option may relate to the most expensive tactic in your marketing plan. Whatever the reasons, if it's important, get to grips with it.

4. Utilising software where possible

Lots of commercial tools exist for the purposes of monitoring your marketing, ranging from Google Analytics (website analysis) and Klout (social media scoring) to MailChimp (email marketing statistics) and Moat (online brand advertising reviews). Some are free to use too. If you have the cash, paid-for versions and chargeable software (such as DataXu) can be utilised for more in-depth studies.

5. Mastering the full range of metrics

Customer acquisition cost, percentage of customers generated by marketing, brand awareness, organic search ranking, net promoter score / customer satisfaction, conversion ratio, marketing mix modelling, social media mentions, communications share of voice, customer lifetime value… the list is endless. Select your metrics wisely or you'll have too many statistics than you know what to do with!

For most firms and chambers the key metric is overall ROI. How much did we spend and what was generated as a result?

In order to obtain these results there needs to be clear logging of all instructions coming into the business including determining if they are brand new instructions or if they are repeat instructions. If they are brand new, where did they come from? Why did they come to you? Can you tie them back to a specific offer or campaign? The only way to know that for sure is to ask the person instructing and then make a note (in the correct database field) so it can be analysed later. It may be, for example, that the new instruction came from a 'family law campaign' and in particular an offer that was placed on social media sites. By logging the granular detail of the origin you can start to understand where the work is coming from and what marketing elements are working and where additional spend might be allocated for greater impact.

By demonstrating success in marketing spend, you are better placed to ask for increased budget next time round with the confidence that you can increase revenue as a result.

Conclusion

Key takeaways from this chapter:-

1. Marketing is NOT a corporate overhead, it is a necessity not a luxury, it's a financial investment that needs to generate a return that can be measured and monitored.

2. Your marketing budget forms an integral part of your marketing plan, allocating monies to all of your proposed activities, for example campaigns, advertising, events and PR.

3. Without a solid budget, you can easily accidentally overspend on marketing costs so it's a control mechanism. Similarly, you can underspend which may have a disastrous impact on your revenues.

4. By taking a logical approach to marketing, backed-up with hard facts you can justify any requests for increased investment.

5. Three approaches to budget setting are commonly used: top down, bottom up or projected return on investment.

6. Three essential steps to help you organise your budgets are; analysis of current finances, determination of spend and the ability to make strategic adjustments throughout the year.

7. Without detailed analysis of your campaigns and events, you're unable to quantify the best and worst exercises, and you may not be investing in those which deliver the highest return on investment for your law firm / chambers.

8. Marketing metrics are key to analysing performance and maximising return on investment.

CHAPTER TEN
PREPARING FOR GDPR

General Data Protection Regulation, or GDPR for short, comes into force on 25th May 2018. Implemented at the same time as the revised Data Protection Bill and updated Privacy & Electronic Communications Regulations, GDPR is the new heavy-duty data protection regime which has four primary aims:-

1. Empower individuals, called 'data subjects', to have more control over their personal data.

2. Hold the organisations collecting, storing and processing data, called 'data controllers' and 'data processors', fully accountable.

3. Harmonise data protection laws across EU member states for a consistently applied approach.

4. Bring current outdated rules up-to-date in order to reflect the huge technological advances that have taken place in the interim period.

If you think GDPR doesn't apply to you because you operate solely in the B2B sector and we're due to leave the EU soon anyway, you're wrong on both fronts. First GDPR applies if you hold any information relating to an identifiable person, including work email addresses, as these can be traced back to an individual.

Second, GDPR applies if you handle personal data for EU citizens. Even when we're outside the EU, if your clients or prospects are inside the EU, you're subject to GDPR rules. Even post-Brexit and even if all your clients or prospects are UK-based, it's likely GDPR and the Data Protection Bill will be combined into one piece of legislation so there really is no getting away from it.

You can be forgiven for being confused about GDPR. It's a hefty piece of legislation which has taken 4 years to negotiate at EU level, comprises 99 articles of law and 173 background paragraphs, called 'recitals', which are explanations of the articles.

There's a lot at stake for abusing data and not implementing enough safeguards to protect it which could result in a security breach. Under the Data Protection Act (DPA), the biggest fine is £500,000. Under GDPR, this rises to a staggering €20 million or 4% of global annual turnover, whichever is greater. Fines imposed are intended to be 'effective, proportionate and dissuasive'.

Aside from these obvious monetary deterrents, your business's professional reputation is at risk too. Public naming and shaming will take place by our supervisory authority. In our country's case, this is the Information Commissioner's Office (ICO). Plus there's the potential for legal actions by affected individuals seeking recompense for material losses and mental distress, which could lead to even more financial sanctions and reputational damage. Of course, for you, as a legal service provider, this is an opportunity in terms of a new source of leads.

With all this in mind, we're going to simplify GDPR by explaining why it's come about, highlighting the main differences to the DPA, defining key terminology and, most importantly, giving you an action plan as to how to get GDPR-ready in your law firm or barristers' chambers. Our action plan contains sample wording for various GDPR collateral.

Reasons for GDPR

But before all that, what's the reasoning behind GDPR? The digital landscape has changed dramatically since 1998 when the DPA was first introduced. Back then, there was no LinkedIn (founded 2002), Facebook (2004), YouTube (2005), Twitter (2006) and even Google was in its infancy. The volume of personal data and the range of channels available to marketers have grown way beyond expectations.

Irresponsible marketing has led to widespread abuse of personal data. In turn, this has led to mistrust in the marketing industry. GDPR shows that it's time to take into account current and future technology trends, address the imbalance of power between marketers and data subjects, allow individuals to decide how their data's used and regain trust in marketing.

On a related note, technology developments also mean cyberattacks have increased in number and sophistication. Personal data is valuable to cybercriminals intent on either partaking in identity theft or causing mayhem just for the fun of it. GDPR recognises that it's time to combat this by implementing watertight security measures that are near-to-impossible to bypass.

Then there's the issue of inconsistent application of data protection rules throughout Europe which currently can be interpreted in vastly varying ways. GDPR emphasises that it's time to introduce one set of prescriptive rules for everyone for a uniform approach to data protection.

Main differences between the DPA and GDPR

There are some similarities regarding the overriding principles – albeit with a new emphasis on transparency and accountability – and terminology used between these two sets of rules. The primary changes under GDPR are:-

- Expanded definitions – personal data now includes an extensive range of online identifiers such as IP addresses; sensitive data, called special categories, also exist and should be treated with extra-special care.

- Wider geographic scope – taking into account the location of both the data controller / data processor and data subject.

- Stronger individual rights – including the right to be informed, right of access, right to rectification, right to object (to direct marketing, automated decision making and profiling), right to erasure and right to data portability.

- Accountability's an obligation – covering technical and organisa-tional measures which are part-and-parcel of privacy by design and default.

- Liability of data processors – those processing data on behalf of data controllers have direct compliance obligations and can face fines too for improper handling or data loss.

- Higher fines – these are €20 million or 4% of global annual turnover, remember?

- Unambiguous consent – gone are the days of pre-ticked boxes and lengthy, complicated legalese; consent should be 'freely given', 'spe-cific', 'informed' and 'unambiguous' based on a 'clear, affirmative action'; another requirement is that consent should be separate from other terms and conditions.

- Mandatory breach notification – you must report serious breaches to the ICO or relevant supervisory authority within 72 hours; if the 'rights and freedoms of individuals' are at risk, you must also inform those affected, ideally with practical help on how they can take action to protect themselves.

- Appointment of a Data Protection Officer – needed for large scale monitoring (if you employ more than 250 employees), processing of highly sensitive data and for public bodies.

- Subject access requests are free – expect to see the number of requests increase because of this; fees can only be charged if addi-tional copies are requested.

Key terminology in GDPR

We've already mentioned data subjects (individuals on whom data is held), data controllers (companies / individuals deciding purposes for which data is processed) and data processors (companies / individuals handling data on behalf of data controllers). Some other useful-to-know terminology is:-

- Lawful grounds for processing – legitimate interests, consent, contract, legal obligation, vital interests or public interest; find out more on each of these at https://ico.org.uk/for-organisations/guide-to-the-general-data-protection-regulation-gdpr/lawful-basis-for-processing.

- Identifiable data – a low bar is now set for this; if a natural person can be identified using 'all means reasonably likely to be used', the information is personal data.

- Special category data – criminal records, religion, health, trade union membership, sexual orientation, racial origin, political beliefs, genetic and biometric data.

- Profiling – any form of automated processing of personal data; profiling by human beings isn't covered.

- Pseudonymisation – substituting the identity of data subjects so that additional, separately stored information is needed for re-identification; this data protection method is strongly advised under GDPR.

- Anonymisation – irreversibly destroys any way of identifying the data subject; GDPR no longer applies when anonymised data's used.

Action plan for GDPR compliance

Now we've hopefully unmuddied the waters a little, we're getting to the finer details of putting GDPR into practice. Just how should you go about preparing for GDPR in your organisation? Here's a list of actions to take both pre and post GDPR go-live:-

<u>Choose your legal basis for processing</u>

Marketers will mainly use legitimate interests and consent. As a general rule of thumb, legitimate interests is more appropriate for existing clients and consent for prospects. As a legal service provider, legal obligation may also come into play. Here's some sample text to communicate the use of legitimate interests processing:-

> *Under data protection legislation, we believe we can demonstrate that we have a legitimate interest in using your data for some marketing purposes but you always have a choice. Please read our privacy policy for more details including how you can opt out of this use of your data.*

The words 'privacy policy' would be hyperlinked on online materials or the full URL provided in offline materials, so individuals can go straight to the privacy policy on your website for more information.

<u>Undertake data mapping</u>

Show, in flow chart format, where data's coming from and who it's going to, by asking yourself questions such as:-

• Where are we getting data from?

• Who are we giving it to?

• Who else has access to it?

• Are we collecting only the information we need?

• What might we do with this data in the future?

This activity will visually highlight any possible weak links in your data management processes as that's all it takes for a major data breach to occur. Rectify these weaknesses at this early stage so it doesn't cause you any problems further down the line.

If you work with third party suppliers, for example providers of practice or chambers management software, ask how they store and process personal data, and ensure proper contractual clauses are in place including data returned or deleted should you decide to terminate your contract.

Audit your data

What personal data do you hold? How did you come about it? If you bought your list, is the data up-to-date and consent valid enough to comply with GDPR? As you're required to keep detailed records of consents and objections to processing, it's likely you'll need to add extra fields added to your CRM database. These could be:-

• I gave consent to processing

• I gave consent to profiling

• This data is processed under legitimate interests

• I objected to direct marketing

• Etc.

Seek new consent

If using consent as your legal basis and you can't show that consent's been given to GDPR standards, seek new and explicit consent as a standalone campaign. Your database will suffer for this but bear in mind that quality's more important than quantity. Thereafter review consent every 2 years, as recommended by the ICO.

Your re-engagement email should cover:-

• Why you're making contact

• How you obtained their personal details

• Type of content you'll send in future if they opt in (make this desirable!)

• How data and communication preferences can be updated

• How they can opt out should they later change their mind

• Link to your privacy policy

<u>Update your privacy policy</u>

The key here is using concise, clear and plain language. Use a layered approach for privacy policies so that readers can access additional information throughout and easily locate what they're looking for. Draw attention to your privacy policy at the point of data collection and remind recipients about it in your first communication.

One of your headings on your privacy policy web page could be:-

What we collect and how we use your data

Clicking on this heading would reveal subtext something to this effect:-

We automatically receive and record information from your computer and browser, including your IP address, software and hardware attributes. We use Google Analytics to track your usage and cookies to remember your preferences.

Return to privacy policy.

Consider just-in-time notices

To be as upfront as possible, set up just-in-time notifications during the various stages of data collection. This could apply to enquiry forms, call-me-back requests, event registrations etc. For example, when capturing data online for a newsletter sign up, as the cursor's clicked in the email address box, pop-up text could advise:-

We use your email address to contact you with important information affecting your industry and advising of changes or developments within our organisation. Please click here to find out more.

Review current data collection processes

You may need to redesign your data capture mechanisms, possibly by introducing double opt in which is considered best practice when using consent as your legal basis. Here's some sample wording for a consent-based registration request:-

At Acme Chambers, we have exciting news about our services and barristers that we hope you'd like to hear about. We will use your information to predict what you might be interested in. We will treat your data with respect and you can find details of our contact promise here. You can stop receiving our updates at any time.

If you'd like to receive marketing from Acme Chambers, please enter your email address here to give your consent: _____

Document how you'll respond to requests from data subjects

Whether this relates to objections to processing or profiling, subject access requests, requests to be erased or requests for data portability, set out exactly what you'll do in each of these scenarios. For the most part, you'll need to action within a 1-month timeframe so it's better to plan ahead now in order to understand what you'll do when the first request arrives.

This may necessitate investment in enhancements to your existing technology or even the purchase of new software to help you handle these new data subject request responsibilities.

Designate data protection contacts

While you may not appoint a Data Protection Officer, you need to allocate someone in a position of seniority the role of ultimate responsibility for data protection compliance. This information (name and contact details) should be included in your privacy policy.

Plan how you'll tackle data breaches

Introduce robust safety measures to prevent breaches to the best of your ability as part of your privacy by design approach. Privacy impact assessments (PIAs) should be carried out to identify and reduce privacy risks for your clients and prospects. Templates for PIAs can be downloaded from https://ico.org.uk/media/for-organisations/documents/1595/pia-code-of-practice.pdf.

You also need to plan how you'll report (within 72 hours) breaches to the supervisory authority (ICO) and subsequently investigate why it came about so it doesn't happen again. Depending on the extent of the breach, you may also need to inform affected contacts too.

Your letter of this nature should describe what happened in general terms including the date of the incident, categories of personal data involved and what you're doing in response. Ideally, it should advise how data subjects can protect themselves by recommending they place a fraud alert on their credit files and change their online banking passwords.

Determine your supervisory authority

Wherever your company's marketing activities are headquartered, you fall under that country's supervisory authority. In the UK, this is the ICO. In Germany, it's the LDI NRW. In France, it's the CNIL. You can find out others with a quick Google search.

Check third party systems used are GDPR compliant

Whether this is use of Google Analytics to monitor website activity or bought-in software to track web visitors more closely, you need to be confident that the providers of these tools are complying with GDPR. You will be held accountable if they're not.

Again, study your contracts carefully. These should incorporate GDPR language, be simply written, and specify roles and responsibilities. Details of these business partners should be given in your privacy policy.

Raise awareness internally

Teach all your employees, from your receptionist to directors, about GDPR and its impact. Everyone has a role to play in keeping sensitive information safe. Just not locking your computer screen when you leave your workstation to make a cup of tea or having confidential paperwork on your desk and not locked away in a drawer for others to see is enough to cause a data breach. Employees also need to know how to answer GDPR-related queries.

Conclusion

There's no denying that GDPR is a game-changer for marketers. Responsible, permission-based marketing is the way to go and abuse of personal data is a thing of the past.

GDPR's not all doom and gloom. While your database may very well diminish (possibly drastically), at least you'll be communicating with individuals who have a genuine interest in what you've got to say so your newsletters, mailers, social media posts and other campaigns won't fall on deaf ears. A small captive audience is much preferable to a large unreceptive audience any day.

The other point to note is that GDPR actually presents a unique opportunity for marketers. Companies demonstrating data governance will enjoy goodwill, loyalty, competitive advantage and, ultimately, better revenues. Conversely, companies who badly manage data and experience breaches will lose clients. As a result, their profit margins and shareholder value will suffer for it.

The key takeaways from this chapter are:-

1. GDPR is a break from tradition. The 20-year-old DPA was desperately in need of an overhaul. GDPR is the new, tough data protection regime that's here to stay, like it or not.

2. GDPR will apply to you, regardless of your unique circumstances. Ultimately, it doesn't matter if your clients and prospects are located, and marketing activities are headquartered outside the EU. GDPR is being introduced pre-Brexit and will apply in some similar form post-Brexit.

3. GDPR's not all negative. Yes, your contact database, built up over many years, may never be the same again but communicating with a smaller, interested group of contacts will generate a higher return on your marketing investment.

4. GDPR's a chance to stand out in the crowd. Shout about your GDPR initiatives to the world. If your competitors can't make similar claims to you, it'll give you the competitive edge.

5. The other opportunity relates to your position as a legal service provider. If you don't already offer data protection law as one of your area specialisms, now's the time to consider doing so. With the predicted rise in legal actions from individuals of misused data taking issue with the data controller or processor in question, your caseload will benefit.

6. Don't wait until 25th May 2018 before trying to work out what to do. Preparedness is key so that, when the date comes, compliance is assured.

CHAPTER ELEVEN
ESSENTIAL CHECKLISTS

As you might surmise, this chapter is a collection of checklists that will help you in the course of your marketing (we do love a good checklist). Where possible, we've added sample entries to get you started.

Marketing priorities checklist

All priorities MUST be relevant to the corporate strategy.

Priorities	Goals	Owner	Metrics	Timescales
E.g. Increase brand awareness	Increase the number of people within the target market aware of your brand	Marketing	Snapshot of numbers before and after campaign Measure: actual numbers	6 months
	Increase the number of newsletter subscribers	Marketing	Snapshot of numbers before and after campaign Measure: actual numbers	6 months

SWOT & PEST templates

SWOT

	Strengths (helpful to fulfilling your strategy)	Weaknesses (harmful to your strategy)
Internal (inside your firm)	• • • • • • •	• • • • • • •
	Opportunities	Threats
External (outside your firm)	• • • • • • •	• • • • • • •

PEST

Political	Economic
· E.g. Legislative changes · · · · · ·	· E.g. Brexit · · · · · ·
Social	**Technological**
· E.g. Population age · · · · ·	· E.g. Case management / workflow · · · · ·

Marketing strategy checklist

	Activity	Results
Services supplied	e.g. Conveyancing	Average matter value £ Average profit per matter £ Profitable or not? Y/N
Target market	Name the target market for each practice area	Number of client and potential clients and indication of quality of data
Communications	How will you communicate with each target market?	Frequency and estimated cost of each type of communications
Events	Type of events (physical and virtual)	Frequency and estimated cost of each

Brand guidelines checklist

Activity	Example	Notes
Email addresses, signatures and business cards	Clear, concise and with the relevant social media links and logos.	
Stationery	Fonts, logos, colours, VAT details – use of Word document templates for all staff / members.	
Signage	An array of sizes and uses with correct placement and type of logo.	
Sales / promotional literature	Brochures, services sheets, case studies, proposals – again these need to have pre-determined and correct placement of logos.	
Advertising	Supply examples of the types of advertisements and the style of font, sentiment, contact details and logo placement.	
Exhibition and display material	Consider what you are using it for and how it will carry the details clearly.	
PowerPoint presentations	Create templates with consistent branding so that anyone can just add their content. Consider having a 'corporate' slide set that details the headline figures / propositions of your whole organisation. The advantages here are	

	consistency of corporate information without limiting the creativity of the individual presentation.	
Corporate clothing and gifts	These need to be in keeping with the values of your brand as well as carrying the corporate colour and logo.	
Mailings	Consider the many different types of formats and how the brand can be represented consistently across all formats.	
Internal staff communications	The branding must be consistent at all times, including in internal communications.	
Press releases	Create a 'boilerplate' for your business. This is a standard paragraph of text that clearly and concisely explains what you do, for whom and where. The boilerplate fits into the bottom of any press release so that editors may pull information from there as required.	

Emailer checklist

Activity		Notes
Who is it from?	Emails from personal email addresses stand a much greater chance of being opened.	
Subject line	80% of your email's success is attributed to the subject line. Provide a reason for reading the rest of the content. Avoid spam words and caps lock (you're not Donald Trump).	
Preview header space	Give a sneak peek into your email and encourage them to read on.	
Personalise	Use your recipient's first name and utilise the words "you" and "your" throughout.	
Jump to the point	Keep it short sweet and simple. Email readers get bored quickly.	
Main section	It must be about how you can help them. Use bullet points where possible.	
Benefits	Focus on the benefits to them and possible risk avoidance.	
Language	Don't be too formal or technical. The reader needs to 'hear your voice'.	

URLs	In your signature or footer section, incorporate hyperlinks to your website, blog or portfolio.	
Calls to action	Make it clear what they should do next.	
E-cards	Only use these where appropriate; Christmas cards etc.	
Test and analyse	Test different content, times, days, subject lines etc. and see what works best for your audience.	
Maximise your content	Re-purpose similar emails on the same theme, saving time and ensuring the message is consistent.	

Direct mail checklist

Activity		Notes
Data	Analyse what you have, buy in from reputable dealers only and cleanse prior to sending.	
Personalise	Tailor to the recipient (not Sir / Madam) and utilise the words "you" and "your" throughout.	
Segmentation	Segmenting your lists into areas enables you to personalise and increase your response rates.	
Landing pages	Create landing pages for your campaign with easy to type URLs or use QR codes within the mailer.	
Craft your message	The more you can hand craft for a specific person or group, the better the response rate will be.	
Be creative	Consider enclosures for added weight and interest.	
Open with a bang	Don't build up excitement towards your value proposition, open with it. Get the reader's attention from the word go and they're more likely to read on.	

Calls to action	Make it clear what they should do next. Make it easy for them to respond.	
Timing	Do NOT send mailers on Fridays – they will arrive in Monday morning's post and will inevitably be 'filed' away with the junk mail.	
Plan, write and edit	Divide into sections and edit as if they only have two minutes to read it. Keep it simple and beneficial to them.	
Design	Make sure the end result in eye-catching but not distracting. Make sure the reader's eye is drawn to benefits and the call to action.	

Social media checklists

Activity		Notes
LinkedIn	• Strategic objective • Creation of a group • Add regular content / thought leadership articles • Identify other groups / people to follow and participate • Encourage participation • Monitor and participate in Q&As • How many posts weekly?	
Facebook Company Page	• Insert strategic objective • Share a mix of relevant links, engaging content, videos and polls • Promote upcoming events (create them in the events tab) • X posts per day • Engage with influencers	
Google+	• Optimize for SEO • X posts per day • Share engaging content, videos, images and relevant links • Comment on posts • Utilise Google Hangouts • Create and promote upcoming events	

| Twitter | <ul><li>Create company identity</li><li>Part of the company culture</li><li>Follow other businesses, thought leaders, clients and partners</li><li>Re-tweet relevant content and news</li></ul> | |

Event checklist

ITEM	ENTER SPECIFIC DETAILS OR TYPE "YES" IF ITEM HAS BEEN SORTED OR "N/A"	ENTER ASSOCIATED COST OR "N/A"	ENTER DATE COMPLETED OR "N/A"
Event title			
Theme of event			
Key note session			
Date(s) & time(s) of event			
Advertising, press (consider sending release to legal publications) and / or listings on website			
Invitations / mailer sent to clients, prospects or attendee list (if provided by event organiser)			
Messaging: what key products are being promoted and what are your messaging statements?			
Agenda			

Location (including full postal address & telephone)			
Venue contact for event (name, email & telephone)			
Map / directions to venue (including details of nearest train / tube stations)			
Welcome signs (for venue reception area)			
Travel arrangements			
Accommodation (including full postal address of hotel & telephone)			
Map / directions to hotel (including details of nearest train / tube stations)			
Staff involved			
Staff rotas (including details of cover times, handover, refreshment & meal breaks)			

Dress code			
Staff instructions re checking in to venue			
Exhibitor / sponsorship guidelines (provided by the event organiser and / or venue)			
Event organiser contact (name, email & telephone)			
Literature for delegate packs (if part of deal)			
Courier delivery date, time & place			
Courier collection date, time & place			
Stand set up time(s)			
Stand break down time(s)			
Exhibition equipment (display stand, pop-ups etc)			
Collateral (brochures, datasheets, case studies etc)			

PowerPoint presentations for laptops / screens			
Giveaways (branded goods such as pens, coasters, gimmicks etc)			
Prize draw (including promo-tional signs & actual prize)			
Lead forms			
Stationery (pens, stapler, paper clips, business cards, return courier labels etc)			
IT & multimedia equipment (laptops, screens etc)			
Electrical equipment (cables, extension leads etc)			
Furniture (liter-ature holders, table(s), seat(s) etc)			
Hire company involvement (for IT equipment and / or furniture)			

Hire company contact for event (name, email & telephone)			
Catering (drinks & glasses)			
WiFi access			
Name badges			
Insurance			
Contingency plans (staff back-up in case of unexpected illness etc)			
Follow-up activity (respond to leads generated)			
Thank you mailer with reminder of next event planned			

Invitation checklist

Activity	Actions	Notes
Design	All materials to have the same design and branding	
Save the date	Send as soon as you have booked the venue	
Invitation	Send 6 weeks before the event	
Keep it simple	• Date • Venue (with map if necessary) • Personalise • Benefits of attending • How to respond (make it easy to respond) • Landing page creation • Easy URL or QR code • Dress code • Data capture method	

Creating customer case studies

Section	Actions	Notes
Client profile	Key contact name Title Direct line Email Company / Client Name Address Tel Fax Web URL Twitter	
Company profile	Number of staff Turnover What does the company do? How long have they been in business? What are their USPs?	
The issue	What was their problem? Why did they need your services? An overview of the case / matter	
The solution	What services did they use? Who supplied them (all team members)?	
The results	What was the outcome of the case?	

| Recommend-ation | Would they recommend your firm / set? What would they tell others? Include team members and set / firm quotes | |

Budget planning checklist

Activity	Q1	Q2	Q3	Q4	Budget	Actual	Variance
National marketing Banner ads							
Local marketing Newspaper ads Radio / TV ads							
Public relations Events Sponsorship Webinars Conferences Client events							
Social marketing Sponsoring content Copywriters (external) Social adverts or boosted posts							
Online Website costs Newsletter / emailer costs App development PPC advertising SEO monitoring							

Market research Client survey Prospect survey Impact studies							
Marketing campaigns Campaign 1 Campaign 2 Campaign 3							
Misc Collateral production Brochures Business cards Stands etc.							

MORE BOOKS BY
LAW BRIEF PUBLISHING

A selection of our other titles available now:

'A Practical Guide to Advising Schools on Employment Law' by Jonathan Holden
'Certificates of Lawful Use and Development: A Guide to Making and Determining Applications' by Bob Mc Geady & Meyric Lewis
'A Practical Guide to the Law of Dilapidations' by Mark Shelton
'A Practical Guide to the 2018 Jackson Personal Injury and Costs Reforms' by Andrew Mckie
'A Guide to Consent in Clinical Negligence Post-Montgomery' by Lauren Sutherland QC
'A Practical Guide to Running Housing Disrepair and Cavity Wall Claims: 2nd Edition' by Andrew Mckie & Ian Skeate
'A Practical Guide to the General Data Protection Regulation (GDPR)' by Keith Markham
'A Practical Guide to Digital and Social Media Law for Lawyers' by Sherree Westell
'A Practical Guide to Holiday Sickness Claims, 2nd Edition' by Andrew Mckie & Ian Skeate
'A Practical Guide to Inheritance Act Claims by Adult Children Post-Ilott v Blue Cross' by Sheila Hamilton Macdonald
'A Practical Guide to Elderly Law' by Justin Patten
'Arguments and Tactics for Personal Injury and Clinical Negligence Claims' by Dorian Williams
'A Practical Guide to QOCS and Fundamental Dishonesty' by James Bentley
'A Practical Guide to Drone Law' by Rufus Ballaster, Andrew Firman, Eleanor Clot
'Practical Mediation: A Guide for Mediators, Advocates, Advisers, Lawyers, and Students in Civil, Commercial, Business, Property, Workplace, and Employment Cases' by Jonathan Dingle with John Sephton
'Practical Horse Law: A Guide for Owners and Riders' by Brenda Gilligan

'A Comparative Guide to Standard Form Construction and Engineering Contracts' by Jon Close

'A Practical Guide to Compliance for Personal Injury Firms Working With Claims Management Companies' by Paul Bennett

'A Practical Guide to the Landlord and Tenant Act 1954: Commercial Tenancies' by Richard Hayes & David Sawtell

'A Practical Guide to Personal Injury Claims Involving Animals' by Jonathan Hand

'A Practical Guide to Psychiatric Claims in Personal Injury' by Liam Ryan

'Introduction to the Law of Community Care in England and Wales' by Alan Robinson

'A Practical Guide to Dog Law for Owners and Others' by Andrea Pitt

'Ellis and Kevan on Credit Hire, 5th Edition' by Aidan Ellis & Tim Kevan

'RTA Allegations of Fraud in a Post-Jackson Era: The Handbook, 2nd Edition' by Andrew Mckie

'RTA Personal Injury Claims: A Practical Guide Post-Jackson' by Andrew Mckie

'On Experts: CPR35 for Lawyers and Experts' by David Boyle

'An Introduction to Personal Injury Law' by David Boyle

'A Practical Guide to Claims Arising From Accidents Abroad and Travel Claims' by Andrew Mckie & Ian Skeate

'A Practical Guide to Cosmetic Surgery Claims' by Dr Victoria Handley

'A Practical Guide to Chronic Pain Claims' by Pankaj Madan

'A Practical Guide to Claims Arising from Fatal Accidents' by James Patience

'A Practical Approach to Clinical Negligence Post-Jackson' by Geoffrey Simpson-Scott

'A Practical Guide to Personal Injury Trusts' by Alan Robinson

'Occupiers, Highways and Defective Premises Claims: A Practical Guide Post-Jackson' by Andrew Mckie

'Employers' Liability Claims: A Practical Guide Post-Jackson' by Andrew Mckie

'A Practical Guide to Subtle Brain Injury Claims' by Pankaj Madan
'The Law of Driverless Cars: An Introduction' by Alex Glassbrook
'A Practical Guide to Costs in Personal Injury Cases' by Matthew Hoe
'A Practical Guide to Alternative Dispute Resolution in Personal Injury Claims – Getting the Most Out of ADR Post-Jackson' by Peter Causton, Nichola Evans, James Arrowsmith
'A Practical Guide to Personal Injuries in Sport' by Adam Walker & Patricia Leonard
'A Practical Guide to Marketing for Lawyers' by Catherine Bailey & Jennet Ingram
'The No Nonsense Solicitors' Practice: A Guide To Running Your Firm' by Bettina Brueggemann
'Baby Steps: A Guide to Maternity Leave and Maternity Pay' by Leah Waller
'The Queen's Counsel Lawyer's Omnibus: 20 Years of Cartoons from the Times 1993-2013' by Alex Steuart Williams

These books and more are available to order online direct from the publisher at www.lawbriefpublishing.com, where you can also read free sample chapters. For any queries, contact us on 0844 587 2383 or mail@lawbriefpublishing.com.

Our books are also usually in stock at www.amazon.co.uk with free next day delivery for Prime members, and at good legal bookshops such as Hammicks and Wildy & Sons.

We are regularly launching new books in our series of practical day-to-day practitioners' guides. Visit our website and join our free newsletter to be kept informed and to receive special offers, free chapters, etc.

You can also follow us on Twitter at www.twitter.com/lawbriefpub.

Printed in Great Britain
by Amazon